GOOD FOOD
I D E A S

Introduction

The trend in today's cooking is towards recipes that are not only fast and easy to prepare but also nutritious and great tasting. With this in mind, the Kraft Kitchens have developed 108 delicious recipes and are bringing them to you in this book.

Each of these recipes has been tested and retested to make sure you will be satisfied with each one you try. You will love the creative entertaining ideas as well as the simple, down-to-earth, family recipes that are included. Paging through this book gives you an idea of all the incredible dishes that you can prepare using versatile Miracle Whip salad dressing. These recipes are designed for almost every need and occasion: for young and old, families and singles, two-career households, and dinner and holiday guests.

Miracle Whip's blend of select ingredients is the key to each and every one of these recipes and is what makes them taste so great. Miracle Whip, which was originally thought of as only an ingredient for salads or as a spread for sandwiches, has become an accepted ingredient for cooking, suitable for many recipes. Miracle Whip salad dressing can even be substituted for mayonnaise in any recipe to make it more special. Today, Miracle Whip salad dressing is an indispensable ingredient used by families everywhere.

Also, Miracle Whip's great taste makes sense from a health standpoint. Miracle Whip salad dressing has 36% less fat and 30% fewer calories than mayonnaise. And, it's low in cholesterol. So, try cooking with the great taste that makes sense.

A Word About the Timings for the Recipes

To aid you in organizing your meals, each recipe gives a preparation time and may give a baking, cooking or broiling time. All times are rounded up to the nearest 5 minutes. The preparation times are based on the amount of time required to assemble the recipe before baking, cooking, chilling, freezing or serving. These times include preparation steps, such as chopping, mixing, cooking rice, pasta, vegetables, etc. If an ingredient can be purchased prepared, such as cooked chicken from a deli, the preparation time will not include the time it takes to prepare that particular food item. The baking, cooking or broiling times are based on the maximum cooking times plus any standing time.

Many of the recipes in this book give microwave directions. Since microwave ovens vary in wattage, our home economists test recipes in standard household microwave ovens measuring 500, 600 and 700 watts. Cooking times should be used as a guideline—check for doneness before increasing the cooking time. Lower wattage microwave ovens may require longer cooking times. Cooking times may also vary as a result of food temperatures, shapes and weight.

Cold
Appetizers

Entertaining is made
easy with this
wonderful variety of
dips, spreads and
finger foods. Many of
these special treats
can be whipped up in
less than 15 minutes
and are great for family
snacking. Pictured here
is Pesto-Layered
Spread; see page 6 for
recipe.

Pesto-Layered Spread

1 envelope unflavored gelatin
1/4 cup cold water
1/2 cup MIRACLE WHIP Salad
   Dressing
1 8-oz. pkg. PHILADELPHIA
   BRAND Cream Cheese,
   softened
2 tablespoons fresh prepared
   pesto
1/2 cup chopped walnuts, toasted

Combine gelatin and water in small saucepan; let stand 1 minute. Stir over low heat until dissolved; cool slightly. Gradually add gelatin to salad dressing, mixing until well blended. Reserve 2 tablespoons gelatin mixture; gradually add remaining gelatin mixture to cream cheese, mixing until well blended. Combine reserved gelatin mixture and pesto; mix well. Layer one-third cream cheese mixture in lightly oiled 5 1/2×3-inch loaf pan or 2-cup mold; cover with half of pesto mixture. Repeat layers, ending with cream cheese layer. Sprinkle with walnuts; press lightly into cream cheese mixture. Chill until firm. Unmold onto serving plate. Serve with toasted French bread slices. Makes 1 1/2 cups.

Preparation time: 15 minutes plus chilling

Variation: Substitute 2-cup bowl for loaf pan; do not unmold.

Recipe tip: For easy removal of spread, line loaf pan or mold with plastic wrap before filling.

Creamy Spinach Dip

1 10-oz. pkg. frozen chopped
   spinach, thawed, well
   drained
1 cup MIRACLE WHIP Salad
   Dressing
1 cup sour cream
1/2 cup chopped parsley
1/4 cup green onion slices
1 teaspoon dill weed
1/2 teaspoon lemon pepper

Combine ingredients; mix well. Cover; chill. Serve with assorted vegetable dippers. Makes 2 1/2 cups.

Preparation time: 10 minutes plus chilling

Variations: Substitute plain yogurt for sour cream.

Substitute MIRACLE WHIP Light Reduced Calorie Salad Dressing for Regular Salad Dressing.

Guacamole Dip

1 ripe avocado, peeled, mashed
1/2 cup chopped tomato
1/4 cup MIRACLE WHIP Salad
   Dressing
2 tablespoons chopped onion
1/4 teaspoon salt
   Dash of hot pepper sauce
2 crisply cooked bacon slices,
   crumbled

Combine ingredients except bacon; mix well. Stir in bacon just before serving. Serve with tortilla chips. Makes 1 1/2 cups.

Preparation time: 15 minutes

Creamy Spinach Dip

Southwestern Appetizer Torte

4 8- to 10-inch flour tortillas
1 ripe avocado, peeled, mashed
1/2 cup MIRACLE WHIP Salad
   Dressing
1/4 cup green onion slices
1/4 teaspoon garlic powder
1 15-oz. can black beans, drained
1 cup chopped tomatoes
   (optional)
1/2 cup chunky salsa
1 4-oz. can chopped green
   chilies, drained
1/2 cup (2 ozs.) 100% Natural
   KRAFT Shredded Sharp
   Cheddar Cheese

Soften tortillas as directed on
package. Combine avocado, 1/4 cup
salad dressing, 2 tablespoons
onions and garlic powder; mix well.
Place one tortilla on serving plate;
cover with beans and second
tortilla. Top with avocado mixture,
third tortilla, tomatoes, salsa and
last tortilla. Cover with combined
remaining salad dressing and
chilies. Sprinkle with cheese and
remaining onions. Makes 10
servings.

Preparation time: 20 minutes

Creamy Dill Dip

1 cup MIRACLE WHIP Light
   Reduced Calorie Salad
   Dressing
2 tablespoons finely chopped
   onion
1 tablespoon milk
1 teaspoon dill weed

Combine ingredients; mix well.
Cover; chill. Serve with vegetable
dippers. Makes 1 cup.

Preparation time: 5 minutes plus
chilling

Variation: Substitute 1 tablespoon
chopped fresh dill for 1 teaspoon
dill weed.

Vegetable Pizza

1 8-oz. can PILLSBURY
   Refrigerated Quick Crescent
   Dinner Rolls
1 8-oz. pkg. PHILADELPHIA
   BRAND Cream Cheese,
   softened
1/2 cup MIRACLE WHIP Salad
   Dressing
1/2 teaspoon Italian seasoning
3/4 cup chopped red pepper
3/4 cup chopped radishes
1/2 cup pitted ripe olive slices
2 tablespoons green onion slices
1/2 cup (2 ozs.) 100% Natural
   KRAFT Shredded Sharp
   Cheddar Cheese

Unroll dough into two rectangles.
Place in 13×9-inch baking pan.
Press onto bottom and 1/4 inch up
sides of pan to form crust. Seal
perforations. Bake at 375°, 10
minutes. Cool. Combine cream
cheese, salad dressing and
seasoning; mix well. Spread over
crust. Top with remaining
ingredients. Cover; chill. Cut into
squares to serve. Makes
approximately 2 dozen.

Preparation time: 20 minutes plus
chilling

Southwestern Appetizer Torte

Shrimp Spread

1 8-oz. pkg. PHILADELPHIA BRAND Cream Cheese, softened
1/2 cup MIRACLE WHIP Salad Dressing
1 4 1/4-oz. can tiny cocktail shrimp, drained, rinsed
1/3 cup finely chopped onion
1/8 teaspoon garlic salt

Combine cream cheese and salad dressing, mixing until well blended. Stir in remaining ingredients. Cover; chill. Serve with assorted crackers. Makes 2 cups.

Preparation time: 10 minutes plus chilling

Munching Onion Dip

1 8-oz. pkg. PHILADELPHIA BRAND Cream Cheese, softened
1/2 cup MIRACLE WHIP Salad Dressing
1/4 cup milk
1/3 cup green onion slices
1 teaspoon Worcestershire sauce

Combine cream cheese, salad dressing and milk, mixing until well blended. Stir in remaining ingredients. Cover; chill. Serve with potato chips. Makes 2 cups.

Preparation time: 10 minutes plus chilling

Variation: Add one garlic clove, minced.

Vegetable-Laced Bagelettes

1 cup shredded carrots
1 cup shredded zucchini
2 hard-cooked eggs, finely chopped
1/4 cup MIRACLE WHIP Salad Dressing
1/2 teaspoon salt
1/4 teaspoon pepper
10 LENDER'S Pre-Sliced Frozen Plain Bagelettes, toasted
1 cup alfalfa sprouts

Combine ingredients except bagelettes and sprouts; mix lightly. Top bagelette halves with sprouts and vegetable mixture. Makes 20 appetizers.

Preparation time: 35 minutes

Variation: Substitute MIRACLE WHIP Light Reduced Calorie Salad Dressing for Regular Salad Dressing.

Smooth Cheddar Spread

2 cups (8 ozs.) 100% Natural KRAFT Shredded Sharp Cheddar Cheese
1/3 cup MIRACLE WHIP Salad Dressing
2 tablespoons green onion slices
1/2 teaspoon Worcestershire sauce

Place cheese and salad dressing in food processor work bowl; process until smooth. Add onions and Worcestershire sauce; process 1 minute. Chill. Serve with assorted crackers. Makes 1 1/2 cups.

Preparation time: 5 minutes plus chilling

Variation: Substitute electric mixer for food processor; mix at medium speed until well blended.

Shrimp Spread

Hot Appetizers

Impress family and guests with the delectable treats that follow. Use them as great nibbles for party snacks or as a prelude to whet appetites for the main course. Pictured here is Sombrero Appetizer; see page 14 for recipe.

Sombrero Appetizer

1 lb. ground beef
1/2 lb. VELVEETA Mexican
  Pasteurized Process Cheese
  Spread with Jalapeño
  Pepper, cubed
2/3 cup MIRACLE WHIP Salad
  Dressing
1/4 cup chopped onion

Brown meat; drain. Add remaining
ingredients; mix lightly. Spoon
mixture into 9-inch pie plate. Bake
at 350°, 10 minutes; stir. Continue
baking 5 minutes. Top with
chopped tomatoes, pitted ripe olive
slices and jalapeño pepper, if
desired. Serve with tortilla or corn
chips. Makes 4 1/2 cups.

Preparation time: 15 minutes

Baking time: 15 minutes

MICROWAVE: Crumble meat into
1 1/2-quart microwave-safe casserole.
Microwave on High 4 to 5 minutes
or until meat loses pink color,
stirring every 2 minutes; drain.
Stir in remaining ingredients.
Spoon mixture into 9-inch
microwave-safe pie plate.
Microwave on High 3 minutes or
until thoroughly heated, stirring
after 2 minutes. Stir. Top with
chopped tomatoes, pitted ripe olive
slices and jalapeño pepper, if
desired. Serve with tortilla or corn
chips.

Cheesy Crab Squares

2 8-oz. cans PILLSBURY
  Refrigerated Quick Crescent
  Dinner Rolls
1/2 cup MIRACLE WHIP Salad
  Dressing
2 teaspoons lemon juice
1/8 teaspoon pepper
2 cups (8 ozs.) 100% Natural
  KRAFT Shredded Sharp
  Cheddar Cheese
6 ozs. imitation crabmeat,
  chopped
1/3 cup green onion slices
1 tablespoon chopped parsley

Unroll dough into four rectangles.
Place in 15×10×1-inch jelly roll
pan; press onto bottom and halfway
up sides of pan to form crust. Seal
perforations. Bake at 375°, 10
minutes. Combine salad dressing,
juice and pepper; mix well. Add
cheese, crabmeat, onions and
parsley; mix lightly. Spread over
crust. Continue baking 12 to 15
minutes or until cheese is melted.
Let stand 5 minutes; cut into
squares. Makes approximately 2
dozen appetizers.

Preparation time: 15 minutes

Baking time: 15 minutes plus
standing

Make ahead: Prepare crust as
directed; cool. Cover tightly.
Combine crabmeat mixture as
directed. Cover; chill. Spread
crabmeat mixture over crust just
before baking. Bake at 350°, 15
minutes or until cheese is melted.

Cheesy Crab Squares

Party Chicken Sandwiches

1½ cups finely chopped cooked chicken
1 cup MIRACLE WHIP Salad Dressing
1 4-oz. can chopped green chilies, drained
¾ cup (3 ozs.) 100% Natural KRAFT Shredded Sharp Cheddar Cheese
¼ cup finely chopped onion
36 party rye or pumpernickel bread slices

Combine chicken, salad dressing, chilies, cheese and onions; mix lightly. Cover bread with chicken mixture. Broil 5 minutes or until lightly browned. Serve hot. Garnish as desired. Makes 3 dozen.

Preparation time: 15 minutes

Broiling time: 5 minutes

Variation: Substitute MIRACLE WHIP Light Reduced Calorie Salad Dressing for Regular Salad Dressing.

Hot Swiss and Almond Spread

1 8-oz. pkg. PHILADELPHIA BRAND Cream Cheese, softened
⅓ cup MIRACLE WHIP Salad Dressing
1½ cups (6 ozs.) shredded 100% Natural KRAFT Swiss Cheese
⅓ cup sliced almonds, toasted
2 tablespoons green onion slices
⅛ teaspoon ground nutmeg
⅛ teaspoon pepper

Combine cream cheese and salad dressing, mixing until well blended. Stir in remaining ingredients. Spread mixture into 9-inch pie plate. Bake at 350°, 15 minutes, stirring after 8 minutes. Garnish with additional toasted sliced almonds, if desired. Serve with assorted crackers or party rye bread slices. Makes 2⅓ cups.

Preparation time: 15 minutes

Baking time: 15 minutes

MICROWAVE: Using 9-inch microwave-safe pie plate, prepare recipe as directed except for baking. Microwave on Medium (50%) 6 minutes or until cheese is melted and mixture is warm, stirring after 4 minutes. (Do not overcook.) Stir before serving. Garnish and serve as directed.

Microwave tips: To soften cream cheese, microwave in microwave-safe bowl on Medium (50%) 30 seconds.

To toast almonds, microwave 1 teaspoon PARKAY Margarine in 9-inch microwave-safe pie plate on High 30 seconds or until melted. Add ½ cup sliced almonds; toss lightly. Microwave on High 6 to 8 minutes or until lightly browned, stirring every 2 minutes. Let stand 5 minutes. Reserve 3 tablespoons almonds for garnish.

Party Chicken Sandwiches

Creamy Egg Rolls

1 14-oz. can chop suey
    vegetables, chopped, well
    drained
1 cup chopped imitation
    crabmeat
1/4 cup MIRACLE WHIP Salad
    Dressing
2 teaspoons soy sauce
8 egg roll wrappers
    Oil
    Mustard Sauce (recipe follows)
    Apricot Sauce (recipe follows)

Combine vegetables, crabmeat,
salad dressing and soy sauce; mix
lightly. For each egg roll, spoon
approximately 1/4 cup crabmeat
mixture onto center of each
wrapper; moisten edges of wrapper
with water. Fold one corner over
filling; fold opposite corners over
first fold. Roll remaining corner
over to seal. Fry, in batches, in
1-inch hot oil, 375°, 2 to 3 minutes
or until golden brown on all sides,
turning once. Drain on paper
towels. Prepare Mustard Sauce and
Apricot Sauce. Serve with egg rolls.
Makes 8 servings.

Mustard Sauce

1/4 cup MIRACLE WHIP Salad
    Dressing
1 tablespoon dijon mustard

Combine ingredients; mix well.
Makes 1/4 cup.

Apricot Sauce

1/4 cup MIRACLE WHIP Salad
    Dressing
2 tablespoons KRAFT Apricot
    Preserves

Combine ingredients; mix well.
Makes 1/3 cup.

Preparation time: 15 minutes

Cooking time: 10 minutes

Recipe tip: For a more blended
flavor, prepare sauces ahead of
time. Cover; chill.

Turkey Empanadas

2 cups finely chopped cooked
    turkey or chicken
1/2 cup MIRACLE WHIP Salad
    Dressing
1/2 cup (2 ozs.) 100% Natural
    KRAFT Shredded Sharp
    Cheddar Cheese
2 tablespoons green onion slices
1/8 teaspoon pepper
1 17 1/4-oz. pkg. frozen puff
    pastry, thawed

Combine turkey, salad dressing,
cheese, onions and pepper; mix
lightly. On lightly floured surface,
roll one pastry sheet to 12-inch
square. Cut into nine 4-inch
squares. Spoon approximately 2
tablespoons filling onto center of
each square. Fold diagonally in
half; press edges together with fork
to seal. Repeat with remaining
pastry and filling. Place on
ungreased cookie sheet. Bake at
450°, 12 to 15 minutes or until
golden brown. Makes 18 appetizers.

Preparation time: 35 minutes

Baking time: 15 minutes

*Creamy Egg Rolls with Mustard
Sauce and Apricot Sauce*

Artichoke Appetizers

2 8-oz. cans PILLSBURY
   Refrigerated Quick Crescent
   Dinner Rolls
3/4 cup (3 ozs.) 100% Natural
   KRAFT Shredded Low
   Moisture Part-Skim
   Mozzarella Cheese
3/4 cup (3 ozs.) KRAFT 100%
   Grated Parmesan Cheese
1/2 cup MIRACLE WHIP Salad
   Dressing
1 15-oz. can artichoke hearts,
   drained, finely chopped
1 4-oz. can chopped green
   chilies, drained (optional)

Unroll dough into four rectangles.
Place in 15×10×1-inch jelly roll
pan; press onto bottom and halfway
up sides of pan to form crust. Seal
perforations. Bake at 375°, 10
minutes. Combine remaining
ingredients; mix well. Spread over
crust. Bake at 375°, 15 minutes or
until cheese is melted. Let stand 5
minutes; cut to serve. Garnish with
thin red pepper strips and parsley,
if desired. Makes approximately 3
dozen.

Preparation time: 15 minutes

Baking time: 15 minutes plus
standing

Garden Vegetable Party Pitas

2 pita bread rounds, cut in half
1 cup (4 ozs.) shredded CASINO
   Brand Natural Monterey Jack
   Cheese
1/3 cup MIRACLE WHIP Salad
   Dressing
1/4 cup chopped radishes
1/4 cup green onion slices

Cut each bread half into four
triangles; split triangles in half.
Place on cookie sheet. Bake at
425°, 5 minutes or until edges are
lightly toasted. Combine remaining
ingredients; mix lightly. Spread
onto bread; continue baking 5
minutes or until cheese is melted.
Makes 32 appetizers.

Preparation time: 10 minutes

Baking time: 5 minutes

Variations: Substitute MIRACLE
WHIP Light Reduced Calorie Salad
Dressing for Regular Salad
Dressing.

Substitute 100% Natural KRAFT
Swiss Cheese for CASINO Brand
Natural Monterey Jack Cheese.

Substitute 24 party rye or
pumpernickel bread slices for pita
bread rounds. Place on cookie
sheet. Continue baking as directed.

Artichoke Appetizers

Garden Appetizers

4 cups shredded zucchini
2 cups shredded carrots
1/2 cup flour
3/4 cup MIRACLE WHIP Salad
    Dressing
1 cup (4 ozs.) shredded CASINO
    Brand Natural Monterey Jack
    Cheese
1/2 cup (2 ozs.) KRAFT 100%
    Grated Parmesan Cheese
1/4 cup chopped onion
1 teaspoon dried basil leaves,
    crushed
Dash of pepper
4 eggs, beaten

Combine zucchini, carrots and flour; toss lightly. Add salad dressing, cheeses, onions, basil and pepper; mix well. Blend in eggs. Spread mixture into lightly greased 13×9-inch baking pan. Bake at 375°, 30 to 35 minutes or until set. Cool slightly; cut into squares. Makes approximately 4 dozen.

Preparation time: 15 minutes

Baking time: 35 minutes plus cooling

Baked Potato Spears

3 large baking potatoes
1/4 cup MIRACLE WHIP Light
    Reduced Calorie Salad
    Dressing
Onion salt
Pepper
Parma Dip (recipe follows)
Hearty Barbecue Dip (recipe
    follows)

Cut potatoes lengthwise into wedges. Brush with salad dressing. Season with onion salt and pepper. Place on greased 15×10×1-inch jelly roll pan. Bake at 375°, 50 minutes or until tender and golden brown. Prepare Parma Dip and Hearty Barbecue Dip. Serve with potatoes. Makes 4 servings.

Parma Dip

1 cup MIRACLE WHIP Light
    Reduced Calorie Salad
    Dressing
1/4 cup (1 oz.) KRAFT 100%
    Grated Parmesan Cheese
1/4 cup milk
1 tablespoon chopped chives

Combine ingredients; mix well. Makes 1 1/4 cups.

Hearty Barbecue Dip

1/2 cup MIRACLE WHIP Light
    Reduced Calorie Salad
    Dressing
1/4 cup KRAFT Thick 'n Spicy
    Barbecue Sauce with Honey
2 tablespoons chopped onion
2 tablespoons chopped green
    pepper

Combine ingredients; mix well. Makes 1 cup.

Preparation time: 10 minutes

Baking time: 50 minutes

Recipe tip: For a more blended flavor, prepare dips ahead of time. Cover; chill.

Baked Potato Spears with Parma Dip and Hearty Barbecue Dip

Fruit & Vegetable Salads

The recipes in this chapter are sure to create renewed enthusiasm for salads with your family. Fresh ingredients are the base for most of these colorful side-dish salads. Pictured here is Wild Rice & Pepper Salad; see page 26 for recipe.

Wild Rice & Pepper Salad

1 6-oz. pkg. long-grain & wild rice
1/2 cup MIRACLE WHIP Salad Dressing
2 tablespoons olive oil
1/2 teaspoon black pepper
1/4 teaspoon grated lemon peel
1 cup chopped red pepper
1 cup chopped yellow pepper
1/4 cup 1-inch green onion pieces

Prepare rice as directed on package, omitting margarine. Cool. Combine salad dressing, oil, black pepper and peel; mix well. Add remaining ingredients; mix lightly. Serve at room temperature or chilled. Makes 6 servings.

Preparation time: 35 minutes

Variation: Substitute MIRACLE WHIP Light Reduced Calorie Salad Dressing for Regular Salad Dressing.

Blue Cheese Salad

1 head iceberg lettuce
3/4 cup MIRACLE WHIP Salad Dressing
1 4-oz. pkg. KRAFT Chopped Blue Cheese Crumbles

Cut lettuce into four slices. For each serving, spread lettuce with salad dressing. Sprinkle with cheese. Makes 4 servings.

Preparation time: 5 minutes

Potpourri Fruit Bowl

1/4 cup MIRACLE WHIP Salad Dressing
1/4 cup sour cream
3 tablespoons KRAFT Apricot Preserves
1 tablespoon lemon juice
2 cups cantaloupe balls
1 peach, sliced
1 cup strawberry halves
1 cup grapes

Combine salad dressing, sour cream, preserves and juice; mix well. Cover; chill. Combine fruit; mix lightly. Serve with salad dressing mixture. Makes 4 servings.

Preparation time: 20 minutes plus chilling

Variations: Prepare salad dressing mixture as directed. Cut one cantaloupe in half horizontally; remove seeds. Scoop out melon balls, leaving shells intact. Combine fruit; mix lightly. Cut edge of shells in zig zag design, if desired. Fill with fruit mixture. Serve with salad dressing mixture.

Substitute MIRACLE WHIP Light Reduced Calorie Salad Dressing for Regular Salad Dressing and plain yogurt for sour cream.

Potpourri Fruit Bowl

Zippy Bean Salad

- 1/2 cup MIRACLE WHIP Salad Dressing
- 1 16-oz. can kidney beans, drained, rinsed
- 1 9-oz. pkg. frozen cut green beans, thawed, drained
- 1/2 cup celery slices
- 1/2 cup onion rings
- 2 tablespoons vinegar
  Few drops hot pepper sauce
  Salt and black pepper
- 4 crisply cooked bacon slices, crumbled

Combine salad dressing, beans, celery, onions, vinegar and hot pepper sauce; mix lightly. Season with salt and black pepper to taste. Cover; chill. Add bacon just before serving. Makes 6 to 8 servings.

Preparation time: 15 minutes plus chilling

Variations: Omit vinegar. Substitute two 15-oz. cans bean salad, drained, for kidney beans and green beans.

Substitute MIRACLE WHIP Light Reduced Calorie Salad Dressing for Regular Salad Dressing.

Our Basic Waldorf Salad

- 1/2 cup MIRACLE WHIP Salad Dressing
- 1/8 teaspoon ground cinnamon
- 2 cups chopped apple
- 1 cup KRAFT Miniature Marshmallows
- 3/4 cup thin celery slices
- 1/4 cup chopped walnuts, toasted

Combine salad dressing and cinnamon; mix well. Add remaining ingredients except walnuts; mix lightly. Cover; chill. Add walnuts just before serving. Makes 4 to 6 servings.

Preparation time: 10 minutes plus chilling

Variations: Add 8 1/4-oz. can pineapple chunks, drained.

Add 1 cup raisins, dates or seedless grapes.

Add 2 cups chopped cooked chicken, turkey or ham.

Carrot Salad

- 2 cups shredded carrots
- 2 cups chopped apples
- 1/2 cup MIRACLE WHIP Salad Dressing
- 1/2 cup raisins
- 1/2 cup chopped pecans

Combine ingredients; mix lightly. Makes 6 servings.

Preparation time: 15 minutes

Variation: Substitute MIRACLE WHIP Light Reduced Calorie Salad Dressing for Regular Salad Dressing.

Food processor tip: To shred carrots, use shredding disk of food processor.

Zippy Bean Salad

Piña Colada Freeze

1 large ripe banana, mashed
1 20-oz. can crushed pineapple,
   drained
2/3 cup MIRACLE WHIP Salad
   Dressing
2/3 cup cream of coconut
2 cups thawed frozen whipped
   topping

Combine banana, pineapple, salad
dressing and cream of coconut; mix
well. Fold in whipped topping.
Spoon mixture into 9×5-inch loaf
pan; cover. Freeze until firm.
Remove from freezer and place in
refrigerator 30 minutes before
serving. Spoon or scoop into
serving dishes. Sprinkle with
toasted flaked coconut, if desired.
Garnish with fresh fruit. Makes 12
servings.

Preparation time: 10 minutes plus
freezing

Variation: Add ¼ cup rum.

Crunchy Pea Salad

½ cup MIRACLE WHIP Salad
   Dressing
¼ cup KRAFT "Zesty" Italian
   Dressing
1 10-oz. pkg. frozen peas,
   thawed, drained
1 cup chopped celery
1 cup peanuts
¼ cup chopped red onion
6 crisply cooked bacon slices,
   crumbled

Combine dressings; mix well. Add
remaining ingredients except
bacon; mix lightly. Cover; chill.
Add bacon just before serving; mix
lightly. Makes 6 to 8 servings.

Preparation time: 15 minutes

Variation: Serve in tomatoes, cut
into six wedges almost to stem end.

Cranberry Waldorf Fluff

1½ cups cranberries, finely
   chopped
1 cup KRAFT Miniature
   Marshmallows
¼ cup sugar
1½ cups finely chopped apple
½ cup MIRACLE WHIP Salad
   Dressing
¼ cup chopped walnuts
⅛ teaspoon ground cinnamon

Combine cranberries, miniature
marshmallows and sugar; mix
lightly. Cover; chill. Add remaining
ingredients; mix lightly. Makes 6
servings.

Preparation time: 20 minutes plus
chilling

Piña Colada Freeze

Walnut-Grape Salad

1/2 cup MIRACLE WHIP Salad
   Dressing
2 tablespoons KRAFT Orange
   Marmalade
2 cups seedless red grapes
1 cup seedless green grapes
1 cup celery slices
3/4 cup chopped walnuts, toasted

Combine salad dressing and
marmalade, mixing until well
blended. Add grapes and celery;
mix lightly. Cover; chill. Stir in
walnuts just before serving. Makes
4 1/2 cups.

Preparation time: 15 minutes plus
chilling

Variations: For main-dish salad,
add 2 cups chopped ham.

Substitute MIRACLE WHIP Light
Reduced Calorie Salad Dressing for
Regular Salad Dressing.

BLT Salad Toss

1 1/2 qts. torn lettuce
1 cup cherry tomato halves
1/2 cup chopped green pepper
6 crisply cooked bacon slices,
   crumbled
1/2 cup red onion rings
1 cup MIRACLE WHIP Salad
   Dressing
1/2 cup (2 ozs.) 100% Natural
   KRAFT Shredded Sharp
   Cheddar Cheese

In 2-quart serving bowl, layer
lettuce, tomatoes, peppers, bacon
and onions. Cover with salad
dressing, spreading to edges of
bowl to seal. Sprinkle with cheese.
Cover; chill. Toss lightly just before
serving. Makes 4 to 6 servings.

Preparation time: 15 minutes plus
chilling

Variations: Substitute MIRACLE
WHIP Light Reduced Calorie Salad
Dressing for Regular Salad
Dressing.

Sun-Sational Lemon Mold

2 cups cold water
1 6-oz. pkg. lemon flavored
   gelatin
1 6-oz. can frozen lemonade
   concentrate
1/2 cup MIRACLE WHIP Salad
   Dressing
1 1/2 cups thawed frozen whipped
   topping
1 11-oz. can mandarin orange
   segments, drained
1 cup blueberries

Bring water to boil. Gradually add
to gelatin, stirring until dissolved.
Add concentrate; stir until melted.
Cool. Gradually add to salad
dressing, mixing until blended.
Cover; chill until thickened but not
set. Fold in whipped topping and
fruit. Pour into 9-inch square pan;
chill until firm. Cut into squares.
Makes 8 to 10 servings.

Preparation time: 2 hours plus final
chilling

Variation: Substitute 2-quart
serving bowl for 9-inch square pan.

Walnut-Grape Salad

Cinnamon-Apple Coleslaw

3 cups shredded green cabbage
2 cups shredded red cabbage
1½ cups chopped apples
1 cup MIRACLE WHIP Salad Dressing
1 tablespoon honey
½ teaspoon ground cinnamon

Combine all ingredients; mix lightly. Cover; chill. Garnish with apple slices, if desired. Makes 6 servings.

Preparation time: 20 minutes plus chilling

Variations: Add ½ cup chopped walnuts, toasted, just before serving.

Honey-Mustard Coleslaw: Omit apples and cinnamon. Add 1 cup shredded carrot and 2 teaspoons KRAFT Pure Prepared Mustard.

Pineapple-Bacon Coleslaw: Omit apples, honey and cinnamon. Add 8-oz. can crushed pineapple, drained, 1 cup shredded carrot and 4 crisply cooked bacon slices, crumbled, just before serving.

Traditional Coleslaw: Omit 2 cups red cabbage; increase green cabbage to 5 cups. Omit apples and honey. Add 1 cup shredded carrot and ¾ teaspoon celery seed.

Substitute MIRACLE WHIP Light Reduced Calorie Salad Dressing for Regular Salad Dressing.

Raspberry-Lemon Gelatin Salad

1 10-oz. pkg. frozen raspberries, thawed
Cold water
1 3-oz. pkg. raspberry flavored gelatin
1 envelope unflavored gelatin
½ cup lemon juice
1 3½-oz. pkg. lemon instant pudding and pie filling mix
2 cups cold milk
1 cup MIRACLE WHIP Salad Dressing

Drain raspberries, reserving liquid. Add enough water to reserved liquid to measure ¾ cup; set aside. Bring 1 cup water to boil. Gradually add to raspberry flavored gelatin, stirring until dissolved. Stir in reserved raspberry liquid. Cover; chill until thickened but not set. Fold in raspberries. Pour into 1½-quart clear serving bowl. Cover; chill until almost set. Combine unflavored gelatin and juice in small saucepan; let stand 1 minute. Stir over low heat until gelatin is dissolved. Cool. Combine pudding mix and milk; mix as directed on package for pudding. Stir in salad dressing. Gradually add gelatin mixture, mixing until well blended. Pour over raspberry layer; cover. Chill until firm. Makes 8 to 10 servings.

Preparation time: 1½ hours plus final chilling

Cinnamon-Apple Coleslaw

Cranberry Holiday Ring

2¼ cups cold water
1 3-oz. pkg. strawberry flavored
    gelatin
1 10½-oz. can frozen cranberry-
    orange relish, thawed
1 8-oz. can crushed pineapple
1 3-oz. pkg. lemon flavored
    gelatin
2 cups KRAFT Miniature
    Marshmallows
½ cup MIRACLE WHIP Salad
    Dressing
1 cup whipping cream, whipped

Bring 1 cup water to boil. Gradually add to strawberry gelatin, stirring until dissolved. Add cranberry-orange relish; mix well. Pour into lightly oiled 6½-cup ring mold; cover. Chill until almost set. Drain pineapple, reserving liquid. Bring remaining water to boil. Gradually add to lemon gelatin, stirring until dissolved. Add marshmallows; stir until melted. Add reserved pineapple liquid; cover. Chill until partially set. Add salad dressing and pineapple to marshmallow mixture. Fold in whipped cream; pour over strawberry layer. Cover; chill until firm. Unmold. Garnish as desired. Makes 12 servings.

Preparation time: 1½ hours plus final chilling

Variations: Substitute 12×8-inch baking dish for ring mold. Do not unmold.

Omit cranberry-orange relish. In 2-quart saucepan, combine 2 cups cranberries, ¾ cup sugar, ½ cup orange juice and 1 tablespoon grated orange peel; bring to boil. Reduce heat. Simmer 10 minutes over medium heat, stirring occasionally. Add to dissolved strawberry gelatin. Continue as directed.

Fruit Cloud

1 cup cold water
1 3-oz. pkg. orange flavored
    gelatin
½ cup MIRACLE WHIP Salad
    Dressing
2 cups thawed frozen whipped
    topping
1 17-oz. can fruit cocktail,
    drained
1 11-oz. can mandarin orange
    segments, drained
1 cup (4 ozs.) 100% Natural
    KRAFT Shredded Sharp
    Cheddar Cheese

Bring water to boil. Gradually add to gelatin, stirring until dissolved. Cool slightly. Gradually add gelatin to salad dressing, mixing until well blended. Cover; chill until thickened but not set, stirring occasionally. Fold in remaining ingredients. Cover; chill. Makes 4 to 6 servings.

Preparation time: 1 hour 15 minutes plus final chilling

Variations: Substitute 1 cup cottage cheese for shredded cheddar cheese.

Substitute 2½ to 3 cups chopped fresh fruit for canned fruit.

Cranberry Holiday Ring

Garden Salad

1/2 cup MIRACLE WHIP Salad
  Dressing
1/4 teaspoon dill weed
2 cups cauliflowerets
1 cup cut green beans
1 cup green pepper chunks
  Salt and black pepper
1 cup cherry tomato halves

Combine salad dressing and dill weed; mix well. Add cauliflowerets, beans and pepper chunks; mix lightly. Season with salt and black pepper to taste. Cover; chill. Stir in tomatoes just before serving. Makes 6 to 8 servings.

Preparation time: 15 minutes plus chilling

Variation: Substitute MIRACLE WHIP Light Reduced Calorie Salad Dressing for Regular Salad Dressing.

Heavenly Seven-Layer Salad

1 1/2 quarts shredded lettuce
2 cups chopped tomatoes
2 cups mushroom slices
1 10-oz. pkg. frozen peas,
  thawed, drained
4 ozs. 100% Natural KRAFT Mild
  Cheddar Cheese, cubed
1 cup red onion rings
2 cups MIRACLE WHIP Light
  Reduced Calorie Salad
  Dressing

In 2-quart serving bowl, layer lettuce, tomatoes, mushrooms, peas, cheese and onions. Spread salad dressing over onions, sealing to edge of bowl; cover. Chill several hours or overnight. Garnish with crisply cooked bacon slices, crumbled, and additional cheddar cheese, shredded, if desired. Makes 8 servings.

Preparation time: 15 minutes plus chilling

Kids' Favorite Fruit Salad

1 orange, peeled, cut into
  4 slices
  Leaf lettuce (optional)
2 medium bananas, cut into
  1/2-inch slices
1/4 cup MIRACLE WHIP Salad
  Dressing
1/2 cup finely chopped peanuts
4 maraschino cherries

For each salad, place one orange slice on lettuce-covered salad plate. Spread one side of each banana slice with salad dressing; dip into peanuts. Arrange bananas, peanut side up, around oranges. Place cherry in center. Makes 4 servings.

Preparation time: 10 minutes

Garden Salad

Potato & Pasta Salads

All-time favorites, potato and pasta salads, take on new twists and contemporary flavors. Try one of these irresistible salads at your next family gathering. Pictured here is Italian Pasta Salad; see page 42 for recipe.

Italian Pasta Salad

1/2 cup MIRACLE WHIP Salad
    Dressing
1/4 cup (1 oz.) KRAFT 100%
    Grated Parmesan Cheese
1/4 cup chopped parsley
2 tablespoons milk
3 ozs. spaghetti, broken into
    thirds, cooked, drained
1 cup salami or ham strips
1 cup carrot slices
1 cup zucchini slices
1/4 cup pitted ripe olive slices

Combine salad dressing, cheese,
parsley and milk; mix well. Add
remaining ingredients; toss lightly.
Cover; chill. Add additional salad
dressing just before serving, if
desired. Makes 4 to 6 servings.

Preparation time: 20 minutes plus
chilling

One Pot Pasta Salad

2 cups (8 ozs.) corkscrew
    noodles
1 16-oz. pkg. frozen broccoli, red
    peppers, bamboo shoots and
    mushrooms
1/2 cup MIRACLE WHIP Salad
    Dressing
1/3 cup KRAFT "Zesty" Italian
    Dressing
1/4 cup (1 oz.) KRAFT 100%
    Grated Parmesan Cheese

Cook noodles as directed on
package, adding vegetables during
last 2 minutes of cooking. Drain;
rinse under cold running water
until cooled. Combine remaining
ingredients; mix well. Add noodles
and vegetables; mix lightly. Serve
at room temperature or chilled.
Makes 4 to 6 servings.

Preparation time: 15 minutes

Variations: Substitute any 16-oz.
pkg. frozen mixed vegetables for
broccoli, red peppers, bamboo
shoots and mushrooms.

Substitute MIRACLE WHIP Light
Reduced Calorie Salad Dressing for
Regular Salad Dressing and
KRAFT "Zesty" Reduced Calorie
Italian Dressing for Regular
Italian Dressing.

Southwestern-Style Potato Salad

3/4 cup MIRACLE WHIP Salad
    Dressing
1 tablespoon chili sauce
1 garlic clove, minced
1/4 teaspoon dried oregano leaves,
    crushed
1/4 teaspoon ground cumin
4 cups cubed cooked potatoes
1 8 1/2-oz. can whole kernel corn,
    drained
1/2 cup diagonally cut green onion
    slices
1/2 cup chopped red or green
    pepper
1/2 cup pitted ripe olive slices
2 tablespoons chopped cilantro

Combine salad dressing, chili
sauce, garlic and seasonings; mix
well. Add remaining ingredients;
mix lightly. Serve at room
temperature or chilled. Garnish as
desired. Makes 6 to 8 servings.

Preparation time: 20 minutes

Variation: Substitute parsley for
cilantro.

Southwestern-Style Potato Salad

Great American Potato Salad

1 cup MIRACLE WHIP Salad
  Dressing
1 teaspoon KRAFT Pure
  Prepared Mustard
1/2 teaspoon celery seed
1/2 teaspoon salt
1/8 teaspoon pepper
4 cups cubed cooked potatoes
2 hard-cooked eggs, chopped
1/2 cup chopped onion
1/2 cup celery slices
1/2 cup chopped sweet pickle

Combine salad dressing, mustard, celery seed, salt and pepper; mix well. Add remaining ingredients; mix lightly. Cover; chill. Makes 6 servings.

Preparation time: 30 minutes plus chilling

Variations: Omit celery and pickle. Add 1½ cups chopped ham and ½ cup chopped green pepper.

Omit celery seed, celery and pickles. Add 1 cup chopped cucumber and ½ teaspoon dill weed.

Omit mustard, celery seed and pickles. Add 3 tablespoons SAUCEWORKS Horseradish Sauce and 1½ cups cubed roast beef.

Pesto Pasta Salad

1/2 cup MIRACLE WHIP Salad
  Dressing
1/2 cup fresh prepared pesto
6 ozs. mostaccioli noodles,
  cooked, drained
2 cups mushroom halves
1 cup red pepper strips

Great American Potato Salad

Combine salad dressing and pesto; mix well. Add remaining ingredients; mix lightly. Cover; chill. Makes 4 to 6 servings.

Preparation time: 20 minutes plus chilling

Summer Pasta Salad

1/2 cup MIRACLE WHIP Light
  Reduced Calorie Salad
  Dressing
1/4 cup (1 oz.) KRAFT 100%
  Grated Parmesan Cheese
2 tablespoons milk
1½ cups chopped cooked chicken
1 cup (4 ozs.) shell macaroni,
  cooked, drained
1 cup cherry tomato halves
1 cup green pepper chunks
2 tablespoons chopped onion
1/2 teaspoon salt

Combine salad dressing, cheese and milk; mix well. Add remaining ingredients; mix lightly. Cover; chill. Add additional salad dressing just before serving, if desired. Makes 4 servings.

Preparation time: 15 minutes plus chilling

Variations: Add ¼ teaspoon dried basil leaves, crushed, to salad dressing mixture.

Omit salt. Substitute ham for chicken.

Seafood Pasta Salad

- ½ cup MIRACLE WHIP Salad Dressing
- ¼ cup KRAFT "Zesty" Italian Dressing
- 2 tablespoons KRAFT 100% Grated Parmesan Cheese
- 2 cups (8 ozs.) corkscrew noodles, cooked, drained
- 1½ cups (8 ozs.) chopped imitation crabmeat
- 1 cup broccoli flowerets, partially cooked
- ½ cup chopped green pepper
- ½ cup chopped tomato
- ¼ cup green onion slices

Combine dressings and cheese; mix well. Add remaining ingredients; mix lightly. Cover; chill. Serve with freshly ground black pepper, if desired. Makes 4 servings.

Preparation time: 15 minutes plus chilling

Variation: Substitute MIRACLE WHIP Light Reduced Calorie Salad Dressing for Regular Salad Dressing and KRAFT "Zesty" Reduced Calorie Italian Dressing for Regular Italian Dressing.

Cucumber-Dill Potato Salad

- ⅔ cup MIRACLE WHIP Light Reduced Calorie Salad Dressing
- ¼ teaspoon salt
- ¼ teaspoon dill weed
- 4 cups cubed cooked potatoes
- 1 cup chopped cucumber
- ¾ cup carrot slices
- 1 tablespoon chopped chives

Combine salad dressing and seasonings; mix well. Add remaining ingredients; mix lightly. Cover; chill. Add additional salad dressing just before serving, if desired. Makes 4 to 6 servings.

Preparation time: 30 minutes plus chilling

Microwave Potato Salad

- 4 cups cubed potatoes
- ⅓ cup cold water
- 1 cup MIRACLE WHIP Salad Dressing
- ⅓ cup KRAFT "Zesty" Italian Dressing
- ¼ cup (1 oz.) KRAFT 100% Grated Parmesan Cheese
- 1 16-oz. pkg. frozen broccoli, green beans, pearl onions and red peppers, thawed
- Salt and pepper

MICROWAVE: Combine potatoes and water in 2-quart microwave-safe casserole; cover. Microwave on High 8 to 12 minutes or until tender, stirring after 6 minutes. Drain. Combine dressings; mix well. Add potatoes, cheese and vegetables; mix lightly. Season with salt and pepper to taste. Cover; chill. Makes 4 to 6 servings.

Preparation time: 20 minutes plus chilling

Variations: Substitute any 16-oz. pkg. frozen mixed vegetables for frozen broccoli, green beans, pearl onions and red peppers.

Substitute MIRACLE WHIP Light Reduced Calorie Salad Dressing for Regular Salad Dressing.

Seafood Pasta Salad

Main-Dish Salads

These memorable main-dish salads tempt your taste buds with their range of savory flavors. The salads in this chapter make a perfect lunch or light dinner meal. Pictured here is Chicken Chutney Salad; see page 50 for recipe.

Chicken Chutney Salad

¾ cup MIRACLE WHIP Salad
    Dressing
¼ cup mango chutney
4 cups cubed cooked chicken
1 cup chopped jicama
1 cup red grape halves
½ cup chopped celery
    Salt and pepper
½ cup coarsely chopped pecans,
    toasted
4 crisply cooked bacon slices,
    crumbled (optional)

Combine salad dressing and
chutney; mix well. Add chicken,
jicama, grapes and celery; mix
lightly. Season with salt and
pepper to taste. Cover; chill. Add
pecans and bacon just before
serving; mix lightly. Serve with
croissants, if desired. Makes 6
servings.

Preparation time: 15 minutes plus
chilling

Pizza Lovers' Salad

½ cup MIRACLE WHIP Salad
    Dressing
½ teaspoon Italian seasonings
1 qt. torn romaine lettuce
1 tomato, chopped
½ cup chopped red or green
    pepper
½ cup sliced mushrooms
½ cup red onion rings
2 ozs. CASINO Brand Natural
    Low Moisture Part-Skim
    Mozzarella Cheese, cubed
½ cup julienne-cut salami
½ cup seasoned croutons

Combine salad dressing and
seasonings in large bowl; mix well.
Add remaining ingredients except
croutons; mix lightly. Serve on
salad plates; top with croutons.
Garnish as desired. Makes 6
servings.

Preparation time: 20 minutes

Northwest Macaroni Salad

½ cup MIRACLE WHIP Salad
    Dressing
2 teaspoons KRAFT Pure
    Prepared Mustard
¾ lb. smoked sausage, cut into
    ¼-inch slices, halved
1 cup (3½ ozs.) elbow macaroni,
    cooked, drained
1 8-oz. can pineapple tidbits,
    drained
⅓ cup chopped green pepper
2 tablespoons chopped onion
    Salt and pepper

Combine salad dressing and
mustard, mixing until well
blended. Add sausage, macaroni,
pineapple, peppers and onions; mix
lightly. Season with salt and
pepper to taste. Cover; chill. Add
additional salad dressing just
before serving, if desired. Makes 4
to 6 servings.

Preparation time: 15 minutes plus
chilling

Pizza Lovers' Salad

Cajun Chicken Salad

3/4 cup MIRACLE WHIP Salad
   Dressing
1 teaspoon ground cumin
1/2 teaspoon ground red pepper
1/8 teaspoon salt
4 cups chopped cooked chicken
1/2 cup chopped celery
1/4 cup chopped red or green
   pepper
2 tablespoons finely chopped
   onion
1 garlic clove, minced

Combine salad dressing and
seasonings; mix well. Add
remaining ingredients; mix lightly.
Cover; chill. Add additional salad
dressing just before serving, if
desired. Makes 4 to 6 servings.

Preparation time: 15 minutes plus
chilling

Variation: Substitute MIRACLE
WHIP Light Reduced Calorie Salad
Dressing for Regular Salad
Dressing.

Nautical Salad

3/4 cup MIRACLE WHIP Salad
   Dressing
1/2 cup sour cream
1/4 cup chopped cucumber
2 tablespoons finely chopped
   onion
2 hard-cooked eggs
1/2 teaspoon dill weed
   Lettuce
2 6 1/2-oz. cans tuna, drained,
   flaked

Combine salad dressing, sour
cream, cucumbers, onions, chopped
egg whites and dill weed; mix well.
Cover; chill. To serve, cover lettuce-
lined salad plate with tuna. Top
with salad dressing mixture and
sieved egg yolks. Garnish as
desired. Makes 4 servings.

Preparation time: 25 minutes plus
chilling

Variations: Substitute MIRACLE
WHIP Light Reduced Calorie Salad
Dressing for Regular Salad
Dressing and plain yogurt for sour
cream.

Substitute one 15 1/2-oz. can salmon
for two 6 1/2-oz. cans tuna.

Recipe tip: To sieve egg yolk, place
yolk in small wire strainer. Using
back of spoon, gently push yolk
through strainer.

Ham & Pasta Salad

2 cups (7 ozs.) medium shell
   macaroni, cooked, drained
1 cup frozen peas, thawed,
   drained
1 cup ham cubes
1/2 cup MIRACLE WHIP Salad
   Dressing
1 hard-cooked egg, chopped
2 tablespoons chopped onion
   Salt and pepper

Combine ingredients except salt
and pepper; mix lightly. Season
with salt and pepper to taste.
Cover; chill. Add additional salad
dressing just before serving, if
desired. Makes 4 to 6 servings.

Preparation time: 25 minutes plus
chilling

Nautical Salad

Jambalaya Salad

1/2 cup MIRACLE WHIP Salad
   Dressing
1/2 teaspoon dried thyme leaves,
   crushed
1/8 teaspoon ground red pepper
1 garlic clove, minced
2 cups cooked rice
1 cup chopped tomato
1 6-oz. pkg. frozen cooked tiny
   shrimp, thawed
1/2 cup ham cubes
1/2 cup chopped green pepper
1/4 cup chopped onion
6 crisply cooked bacon slices,
   crumbled

Combine salad dressing,
seasonings and garlic; mix well.
Add remaining ingredients except
bacon; mix lightly. Cover; chill.
Add bacon just before serving; mix
lightly. Garnish as desired. Makes
4 to 6 servings.

Preparation time: 25 minutes plus
chilling

Layered Taco Salad

4 chicken breast halves, boned,
   skinned, cubed
1 tablespoon oil
3/4 cup salsa
   Guacamole (recipe follows)
3 cups coarsely broken tortilla
   chips
1 qt. torn lettuce
1 15-oz. can kidney beans,
   drained, rinsed
1 cup (4 ozs.) 100% Natural
   KRAFT Shredded Sharp
   Cheddar Cheese
2 crisply cooked bacon slices,
   crumbled

Stir-fry chicken in oil in 10-inch
skillet over medium-high heat 4 to
5 minutes or until tender. Reduce
heat to medium. Stir in salsa;
cover. Simmer 5 minutes. Prepare
Guacamole. In 3- to 4-quart serving
bowl, layer chips, lettuce, beans
and chicken mixture. Cover with
Guacamole, spreading to edges of
bowl to seal. Sprinkle with cheese.
Cover; chill. Add bacon; toss lightly
just before serving. Makes 8
servings.

Guacamole

1 ripe avocado, peeled, mashed
1/2 cup MIRACLE WHIP Salad
   Dressing
1/2 cup salsa

Combine ingredients; mix well.
Makes approximately 1 1/4 cups.

Preparation time: 20 minutes plus
chilling

Microwave tip: Omit oil. To cook
chicken, place chicken in 1 1/2-quart
microwave-safe casserole; cover.
Microwave on High 4 to 5 minutes
or until tender, stirring every 2
minutes. Drain; stir in salsa.
Microwave on High 1 minute.

Jambalaya Salad

Entrees

Variety is highlighted in these appealing main-dish recipes—casseroles, stir-fries, sandwiches, and more, using seafood, poultry, meats and dairy products. There's something for everyone's taste. Pictured here is Crab & Broccoli Frittata; see page 58 for recipe.

Crab & Broccoli Frittata

6 eggs, beaten
1/3 cup MIRACLE WHIP Salad Dressing
1 1/2 cups 100% Natural KRAFT Shredded Sharp Cheddar Cheese
1 cup chopped broccoli, cooked, drained
1 1/2 cups chopped imitation crabmeat
Dash of pepper

Combine eggs and salad dressing; mix well. Stir in 1 cup cheese, broccoli, crabmeat and pepper. Pour into well-greased 9-inch pie plate or 10-inch ovenproof skillet. Bake at 350°, 25 minutes or until set. Top with remaining cheese; continue baking 5 minutes or until cheese is melted. Cut into wedges to serve. Makes 6 servings.

Preparation time: 10 minutes

Baking time: 30 minutes

MICROWAVE: In medium microwave-safe bowl, combine eggs, salad dressing, 1 cup cheese, broccoli, crabmeat and pepper. Microwave on High 2 minutes, stirring after each minute. Pour into 9-inch microwave-safe pie plate or 10×6-inch microwave-safe baking dish. Cover with plastic wrap; vent. Microwave on High 7 to 9 minutes or until almost set, turning dish every 4 minutes. Top with remaining cheese. Let stand, covered, 5 minutes. Cut into wedges to serve.

Fettucini Italiano

8 ozs. fettucini
1/3 cup MIRACLE WHIP Light Reduced Calorie Salad Dressing
1 garlic clove, minced
1/2 cup milk
5 crisply cooked bacon slices, crumbled
1/3 cup (1 1/2 ozs.) KRAFT 100% Grated Parmesan Cheese
1/4 cup chopped parsley

Prepare fettucini as directed on package; drain. Combine salad dressing and garlic in small saucepan. Gradually stir in milk; heat thoroughly, stirring occasionally. Toss with hot fettucini until well coated. Add remaining ingredients; toss lightly. Makes 5 servings.

Preparation time: 25 minutes

Variations: Substitute spaghetti for fettucini.

Substitute MIRACLE WHIP Salad Dressing for Reduced Calorie Salad Dressing.

MICROWAVE: Prepare fettucini as directed on package; drain. Combine salad dressing and garlic in 2-quart microwave-safe bowl; gradually add milk. Microwave on High 1 1/2 to 2 minutes or until thoroughly heated, stirring after 1 minute. (Do not boil.) Add hot fettucini; toss until well coated. Continue as directed.

Fettucini Italiano

Baked Chicken Parmesan

1 cup cornflake crumbs
1/2 cup (2 ozs.) KRAFT 100%
    Grated Parmesan Cheese
Dash of salt and pepper
1 2 1/2- to 3-lb. broiler-fryer, cut
    up, skinned
3/4 cup MIRACLE WHIP Salad
    Dressing

Combine crumbs, cheese, salt and
pepper. Brush chicken with salad
dressing; coat with crumb mixture.
Place in 13×9-inch baking dish.
Bake at 350°, 1 hour or until
tender. Serve with your favorite
accompaniments. Makes 3 to 4
servings.

Preparation time: 15 minutes

Baking time: 1 hour

Variations: For Cajun Chicken,
omit salt. Add 1 teaspoon *each*
ground cumin and onion powder
and 1/2 teaspoon *each* ground red
pepper and garlic powder to salad
dressing; mix well. Substitute 1 1/2
cups crushed sesame crackers for
cornflake crumbs and parmesan
cheese. Continue as directed.

Substitute MIRACLE WHIP Light
Reduced Calorie Salad Dressing for
Regular Salad Dressing.

MICROWAVE: Substitute 12×8-inch
microwave-safe baking dish for
13×9-inch baking dish. Coat
chicken as directed. Arrange in
baking dish with meatiest portions
toward outside of dish. Microwave
on High 17 to 20 minutes or until
chicken is tender, turning dish
after 8 minutes. Let stand 5
minutes. Serve with your favorite
accompaniment.

Swiss Club Bundles

3/4 cup (3 ozs.) 100% Natural
    KRAFT Shredded Swiss
    Cheese
1 cup finely chopped ham
1/2 cup MIRACLE WHIP Salad
    Dressing
1/4 cup green onion slices
2 tablespoons KRAFT 100%
    Grated Parmesan Cheese
4 6-inch French bread rolls,
    partially split

Combine ingredients except rolls;
mix lightly. Fill rolls with ham
mixture; wrap in foil. Bake at
350°, 15 minutes or until
thoroughly heated. Makes 8
sandwiches.

Preparation time: 10 minutes

Baking time 15 minutes

Variations: Substitute hamburger
buns for French bread rolls.

Substitute cooked turkey or
chicken for ham.

Baked Chicken Parmesan

Oriental Pork

1/2 cup MIRACLE WHIP Salad
   Dressing
3 tablespoons peanut butter
1 tablespoon soy sauce
1/2 teaspoon ground ginger
2 tablespoons oil
2 cups diagonally cut celery
   slices
1 red or green pepper, cut into
   chunks
1/4 cup green onion slices
1 garlic clove, minced
1 lb. lean pork, cut into 1/2-inch
   strips
3 cups shredded lettuce

Combine salad dressing, peanut butter, soy sauce and ginger; mix well. Set aside. Heat 1 tablespoon oil in large skillet or wok over medium-high heat 1 minute. Add vegetables and garlic; stir-fry 4 minutes or until crisp-tender. Remove vegetables and garlic from skillet; add remaining oil to skillet. Add pork; stir-fry 9 to 10 minutes or until pork is no longer pink. Return vegetables to skillet. Add salad dressing mixture; mix lightly. Serve over lettuce. Makes 4 servings.

Preparation time: 30 minutes

Cooking time: 20 minutes

MICROWAVE: Omit oil. Combine salad dressing, peanut butter, soy sauce and ginger; mix well. Set aside. Place vegetables and garlic in medium microwave-safe bowl. Cover with plastic wrap; vent. Microwave on High 3 1/2 to 4 minutes or until vegetables are crisp-tender, stirring after 2 minutes. Set aside. Place meat in 2-quart microwave-safe casserole; cover. Microwave on High 5 to 6 minutes or until pork is no longer pink, stirring every 2 minutes; drain. Add salad dressing mixture and reserved vegetables; mix well. Microwave, covered, on High 1 to 2 minutes or until thoroughly heated. Serve as directed.

Zucchini Ham Bake

4 cups thinly sliced zucchini
1 cup sliced mushrooms
1/2 cup onion rings
1 garlic clove, minced
1 teaspoon Italian seasoning
1 egg, beaten
2/3 cup MIRACLE WHIP Salad
   Dressing
1/2 cup sour cream
1 tablespoon flour
2 cups chopped ham
1 cup (4 ozs.) shredded CASINO
   Brand Natural Monterey Jack
   Cheese

Combine zucchini, mushrooms, onions, garlic and seasoning; mix lightly. Combine egg, salad dressing, sour cream and flour, mixing until well blended. In greased 12×8-inch baking dish, layer half the vegetable mixture, salad dressing mixture, ham and cheese; repeat layers. Bake at 350°, 30 minutes or until thoroughly heated. Makes 6 servings.

Preparation time: 20 minutes

Baking time: 30 minutes

Eggplant Rolls

1 10-oz. pkg. frozen chopped
  spinach, thawed, well
  drained
1 cup ricotta cheese
2/3 cup MIRACLE WHIP Salad
  Dressing
1 large eggplant, peeled, cut
  lengthwise into 8 slices
1/2 cup dry bread crumbs
2 to 3 tablespoons oil
1 15 1/2-oz. jar spaghetti sauce
1/2 cup (2 ozs.) 100% Natural
  KRAFT Shredded Low
  Moisture Part-Skim
  Mozzarella Cheese
1/4 cup (1 oz.) KRAFT 100%
  Grated Parmesan Cheese

Combine spinach, ricotta cheese
and 1/3 cup salad dressing; mix
lightly. Brush both sides of
eggplant slices generously with
remaining salad dressing; coat
with crumbs. Heat 2 tablespoons
oil in large skillet over medium-
high heat. Add eggplant, two slices
at a time. Cook over medium heat
until tender and lightly browned,
adding additional oil as necessary.
Spread approximately 1/4 cup
spinach mixture onto each
eggplant slice. Roll up, starting at
narrow end. Place, seam-side down,
in 8-inch square baking dish. Top
with spaghetti sauce and cheeses.
Bake at 350°, 30 minutes or until
thoroughly heated. Makes 4
servings.

Preparation time: 40 minutes

Baking time: 30 minutes

MICROWAVE: Assemble recipe as
directed except for topping with
cheeses. Place, seam-side down, in
8-inch square microwave-safe
baking dish. Cover with wax paper.
Microwave on High 11 to 12

minutes or until thoroughly
heated, turning dish every 4
minutes. Top with cheeses.
Microwave, uncovered, on High 1 1/2
to 2 minutes or until mozzarella
cheese is melted.

Microwave tip: To thaw spinach,
place frozen spinach in 1-quart
microwave-safe casserole; cover.
Microwave on High 3 1/2 minutes.
Break apart with fork; drain well.

Beach Picnic Sandwiches

2 cups shredded cabbage
  MIRACLE WHIP Salad Dressing
1/4 cup chopped green pepper
1/2 teaspoon celery seed
6 hard rolls, split
  Assorted luncheon meat slices
  100% Natural KRAFT Swiss or
  Muenster Cheese Slices, cut
  in half
  Tomato slices

Combine cabbage, 1/4 cup salad
dressing, peppers and celery seed;
mix lightly. Spread rolls with
additional salad dressing; fill with
cabbage mixture, meat, cheese and
tomatoes. Makes 6 sandwiches.

Preparation time: 20 minutes

Variations: Substitute 100%
Natural KRAFT Monterey Jack or
Cheddar Cheese Slices for Swiss or
Muenster Slices.

Substitute lettuce for cabbage, 3
whole-wheat pita bread rounds, cut
in half, for 6 hard rolls, split, and
turkey slices for assorted luncheon
meat slices.

Substitute MIRACLE WHIP Light
Reduced Calorie Salad Dressing for
Regular Salad Dressing.

Tasty Turkey Pot Pie

1/2 cup MIRACLE WHIP Salad
   Dressing
2 tablespoons flour
1 teaspoon instant chicken
   bouillon
1/8 teaspoon pepper
3/4 cup milk
1 1/2 cups chopped cooked turkey
   or chicken
1 10-oz. pkg. frozen mixed
   vegetables, thawed, drained
1 4-oz. can PILLSBURY
   Refrigerated Quick Crescent
   Dinner Rolls

Combine salad dressing, flour,
bouillon and pepper in medium
saucepan. Gradually add milk.
Cook, stirring constantly, over low
heat until thickened. Add turkey
and vegetables; heat thoroughly,
stirring occasionally. Spoon into
8-inch square baking dish. Unroll
dough into two rectangles. Press
perforations together to seal. Place
rectangles side-by-side to form
square; press edges together to
form seam. Cover turkey mixture
with dough. Bake at 375°, 15 to 20
minutes or until browned. Makes 4
to 6 servings.

Preparation time: 15 minutes

Baking time: 20 minutes

Variations: Combine 1 egg, beaten,
and 1 tablespoon cold water,
mixing until well blended. Brush
dough with egg mixture just before
baking.

Substitute one chicken bouillon
cube for instant chicken bouillon.

Substitute 10×6-inch baking dish
for 8-inch square baking dish.

Substitute 12×8-inch baking dish
for 8-inch square dish. Double all
ingredients. Assemble recipe as
directed, using three dough
rectangles to form top crust.
Decorate crust with cut-outs from
remaining rectangle. Bake as
directed.

Microwave tip: To prepare sauce,
combine salad dressing, flour,
bouillon and pepper in 1-quart
microwave-safe measure or bowl;
gradually add milk. Microwave on
High 4 to 5 minutes or until
thickened, stirring after each
minute.

"Just for Kids" Sandwich

1/4 cup MIRACLE WHIP Salad
   Dressing
1/4 cup peanut butter
1/2 cup chopped apple
1/4 cup raisins
8 bread slices

Combine salad dressing and
peanut butter, mixing until well
blended. Stir in apples and raisins.
For each sandwich, spread one
bread slice with salad dressing
mixture; top with second bread
slice. Makes 4 sandwiches.

Preparation time: 10 minutes

Tasty Turkey Pot Pie

Almond-Chicken Casserole

1 cup fresh bread cubes
1 tablespoon PARKAY Margarine, melted
3 cups chopped cooked chicken
1½ cups diagonally cut celery slices
1 cup MIRACLE WHIP Salad Dressing
1 cup (4 ozs.) shredded 100% Natural KRAFT Swiss Cheese
½ cup 1½-inch-long red or green pepper strips
¼ cup slivered almonds, toasted
¼ cup chopped onion

Combine bread cubes and margarine; toss lightly. Set aside. Combine remaining ingredients; mix lightly. Spoon into 10×6-inch baking dish. Top with bread cubes. Bake at 350°, 30 minutes or until lightly browned. Garnish as desired. Makes 6 servings.

Preparation time: 20 minutes

Baking time: 30 minutes

MICROWAVE: Combine bread cubes and margarine in 9-inch microwave-safe pie plate; toss lightly. Microwave on High 2 minutes, stirring after 1 minute; set aside. Combine remaining ingredients in 10×6-inch microwave-safe baking dish. Microwave 3 minutes; stir. Top with bread cubes. Microwave 2 to 3 minutes or until thoroughly heated. Garnish as desired.

Almond-Chicken Casserole

Midwestern Stir-Fry

½ cup MIRACLE WHIP Salad Dressing
2 tablespoons milk
½ teaspoon KRAFT Pure Prepared Mustard
½ lb. smoked sausage, cut into ¼-inch slices, halved
¾ cup yellow squash slices, halved
½ cup green or red pepper strips
½ cup 1-inch green onion pieces
Hot cooked rice

Combine salad dressing, milk and mustard, mixing until well blended; set aside. Stir-fry sausage in large skillet or wok over high heat until thoroughly heated. Remove sausage from skillet; drain, reserving 1 tablespoon fat. Return reserved fat to skillet. Add squash and peppers. Stir-fry 3 minutes. Return sausage to skillet with onions; stir-fry 1 minute. Remove from heat. Add salad dressing mixture; mix lightly. Serve over hot cooked rice. Makes 4 servings.

Preparation time: 10 minutes

Cooking time: 10 minutes

MICROWAVE: Combine salad dressing, milk and mustard, mixing until well blended; set aside. Combine sausage, peppers and onions in medium microwave-safe bowl. Microwave on High 2 minutes. Stir in squash. Continue microwaving on High 2 minutes or until vegetables are crisp-tender. Add salad dressing mixture; mix lightly. Microwave on Medium (50%) 2 to 3 minutes or until thoroughly heated, stirring after 2 minutes. Do not overheat. Serve over hot cooked rice.

Parmesan Turkey Divan

1/4 cup PARKAY Margarine
1/4 cup flour
1 1/2 cups milk
1/3 cup MIRACLE WHIP Salad
    Dressing
2 10-oz. pkgs. frozen broccoli
    spears, thawed, drained
1/2 cup (2 ozs.) KRAFT 100%
    Grated Parmesan Cheese
6 cooked turkey slices, 1/4 inch
    thick (approx. 3/4 lb.)

Melt margarine in saucepan over low heat. Blend in flour. Gradually add milk; cook, stirring constantly, until thickened. Stir in salad dressing. Arrange broccoli in 12×8-inch baking dish; sprinkle with 1/4 cup cheese. Top with turkey, salad dressing mixture and remaining cheese. Bake at 350°, 35 to 40 minutes or until thoroughly heated. Makes 6 to 8 servings.

Preparation time: 20 minutes

Baking time: 40 minutes

Make ahead: Prepare recipe as directed except for baking. Cover with foil; chill. When ready to serve, bake, covered, at 350°, 30 minutes. Remove cover; continue baking 20 minutes or until thoroughly heated.

MICROWAVE: Microwave margarine in 1-quart microwave-safe measure on High 1 minute or until melted. Blend in flour; microwave on High 1 minute. Gradually add milk; microwave on High 4 to 5 minutes or until thickened, stirring well after each minute. Stir in salad dressing. Using 12×8-inch microwave-safe casserole, assemble recipe as directed. Cover with plastic wrap; vent. Microwave on High 8 to 9 minutes or until thoroughly heated, turning dish every 3 minutes.

Easy Ham & Potatoes au Gratin

1 lb. (3 1/2 cups) frozen hash
    brown potatoes, thawed
1 1/2 cups chopped ham
1 cup (4 ozs.) 100% Natural
    KRAFT Shredded Sharp
    Cheddar Cheese
1/2 cup MIRACLE WHIP Salad
    Dressing
1/2 cup milk
1/2 cup fresh bread crumbs
1 tablespoon PARKAY Margarine,
    melted
    Salt and pepper

Combine potatoes, ham and cheese; mix lightly. Combine salad dressing and milk; mix well. Add salad dressing mixture to potato mixture; mix lightly. Spoon into 1-quart casserole. Combine crumbs and margarine; sprinkle over potato mixture. Bake at 350°, 40 to 45 minutes or until thoroughly heated. Season with salt and pepper to taste. Makes 4 to 6 servings.

Preparation time: 10 minutes

Baking time: 45 minutes

Variation: Omit ham. Add ¼ cup chopped onion.

Make ahead: Prepare recipe as directed except for baking. Cover; chill. When ready to serve, remove cover. Bake at 350°, 1 hour or until thoroughly heated.

MICROWAVE: Reduce milk to ⅓ cup. Substitute 1½-quart microwave-safe casserole for 1-quart casserole. Microwave margarine in 1½-quart microwave-safe casserole on High 30 seconds or until melted; stir in crumbs. Microwave on High 2 minutes. Remove from casserole; set aside. Combine remaining ingredients as directed in 1½-quart microwave-safe casserole; cover. Microwave on High 10 to 12 minutes or until thoroughly heated, stirring every 4 minutes. Stir; sprinkle with reserved crumbs. Let stand 5 minutes.

Microwave tip: To thaw potatoes, place potatoes in 1½-quart microwave-safe casserole. Microwave on Medium (50%) 5 to 6 minutes or until thawed, stirring after 3 minutes.

Chicken Dijon

½ cup MIRACLE WHIP Salad Dressing
¼ cup dijon mustard
1 2½- to 3-lb. broiler-fryer, cut up, skinned
1¼ cups dry bread crumbs
¼ cup PARKAY Margarine, melted

Combine salad dressing and mustard, mixing until well blended. Brush chicken with salad dressing mixture; coat with crumbs. Place in 13×9-inch baking dish; drizzle with margarine. Bake at 350°, 1 hour or until chicken is tender. Makes 4 servings.

Preparation time: 25 minutes

Baking time: 1 hour

Variation: Substitute MIRACLE WHIP Light Reduced Calorie Salad Dressing for Regular Salad Dressing.

MICROWAVE: Substitute 12×8-inch microwave-safe baking dish for 13×9-inch baking dish. Add ½ teaspoon paprika to crumbs. Coat chicken as directed. Arrange in baking dish with meatiest portions toward outside of dish; drizzle with margarine. Microwave on High 17 to 20 minutes or until chicken is tender, turning dish after 8 minutes. Let stand 5 minutes.

Pork Piccata

3/4 lb. pork tenderloin
1/2 cup MIRACLE WHIP Salad
    Dressing
1/4 cup seasoned bread crumbs
1 tablespoon KRAFT 100%
    Grated Parmesan Cheese
1 tablespoon PARKAY Margarine
1 garlic clove, minced
1 tablespoon milk
1 tablespoon capers, drained
1 teaspoon lemon juice

Slice pork into 3/4-inch slices;
pound to 1/4-inch thickness. Spread
pork generously with 1/4 cup salad
dressing. Combine crumbs and
cheese. Coat pork with crumb
mixture. Melt margarine. Add
garlic; cook until tender. Reduce
heat. Add pork; cook over medium
heat until meat is no longer pink.
Combine remaining salad dressing,
milk, capers and juice; mix well.
Serve with pork. Serve with your
favorite accompaniments. Makes 4
servings.

Preparation time: 20 minutes

Cooking time: 20 minutes

Country Chicken Bake

1 cup uncooked rice
1 cup celery slices
3/4 cup chopped onion
2 teaspoons parsley flakes
1/8 teaspoon pepper
1 10 3/4-oz. can condensed cream
    of mushroom soup
3/4 cup MIRACLE WHIP Salad
    Dressing
1 3/4 cups cold water
6 chicken breast halves, skinned

Place rice in greased 12×8-inch
baking dish. Combine vegetables
and seasonings; spoon over rice.
Combine soup and salad dressing;
mix well. Gradually add water to
soup mixture, mixing until well
blended. Pour half the soup
mixture over vegetables; top with
chicken and remaining soup
mixture. Bake at 350°, 1 hour or
until chicken is tender and rice is
cooked. Sprinkle with paprika, if
desired. Makes 6 servings.

Preparation time: 15 minutes

Baking time: 1 hour

Variations: Substitute MIRACLE
WHIP Light Reduced Calorie Salad
Dressing for Regular Salad
Dressing.

Substitute boneless chicken breasts
for chicken breasts. Reduce baking
time to 45 minutes or until chicken
is tender.

Pork Piccata

Stuffed Pasta Shells

2 cups finely chopped cooked
  ham or turkey
1 cup ricotta cheese
½ cup MIRACLE WHIP Salad
  Dressing
¼ cup chopped red onion
4 ozs. (18) large pasta shells,
  cooked, drained
2 tablespoons cold water
¼ cup (1 oz.) KRAFT 100%
  Grated Parmesan Cheese
¼ cup dry bread crumbs
1 to 2 tablespoons chopped
  parsley
1 tablespoon PARKAY Margarine

Combine ham, ricotta cheese, salad
dressing and onions; mix lightly.
Fill shells with ham mixture;
place, filled side up, in shallow
baking dish. Add 2 tablespoons
cold water to dish; cover with foil.
Bake at 350°, 30 minutes or until
thoroughly heated. Combine
parmesan cheese, crumbs, parsley
and margarine, melted; sprinkle
over shells. Continue baking,
uncovered, 5 minutes. Serve with
your favorite accompaniments.
Makes 6 servings.

Preparation time: 15 minutes

Baking time: 35 minutes

MICROWAVE: Omit cold water.
Microwave margarine in 9-inch
microwave-safe pie plate on High
30 seconds or until melted. Stir in
parmesan cheese and crumbs.
Microwave on High 2 minutes,
stirring after 1 minute. Stir in
parsley; set aside. Assemble shells
as directed; place in shallow
microwave-safe baking dish. Cover
with plastic wrap; vent. Microwave
on High 7 to 8 minutes or until
thoroughly heated, turning dish
after 4 minutes. Sprinkle with
parmesan cheese mixture. Let
stand 5 minutes. Serve with your
favorite accompaniments.

Gyros Sandwiches

½ lb. gyros meat
4 pita bread rounds
  MIRACLE WHIP Salad Dressing
4 ozs. feta cheese, crumbled
½ cup chopped cucumber
½ cup thin onion slices,
  separated into rings
  Chopped tomatoes

Brown meat. Lightly brush both
sides of bread rounds with salad
dressing. Place on cookie sheet;
sprinkle with cheese. Bake at 350°,
5 minutes. Combine cucumber,
onions and ⅓ cup salad dressing.
Cover bread rounds with meat,
salad dressing mixture and
tomatoes. Fold in half to serve.
Makes 4 sandwiches.

Preparation time: 20 minutes

Stuffed Pasta Shells

Cajun Baked Fish

¹/₃ cup MIRACLE WHIP Salad
 Dressing
¹/₂ teaspoon ground cumin
¹/₂ teaspoon onion powder
¹/₄ teaspoon ground red pepper
¹/₄ teaspoon garlic powder
 1 lb. fish fillets
¹/₂ cup crushed sesame crackers

Combine salad dressing and
seasonings; mix well. Brush fish
with salad dressing mixture; coat
with crumbs. Place in greased
shallow baking dish. Bake at 350°,
30 minutes or until fish begins to
flake when tested with a fork.
Serve with your favorite
accompaniments. Makes 3 to 4
servings.

Preparation time: 15 minutes

Baking time: 30 minutes

MICROWAVE: Combine salad
dressing and seasonings; mix well.
Brush fish with salad dressing
mixture; coat with crumbs.
Arrange fish in shallow microwave-
safe baking dish, placing thickest
portions toward outside of dish.
Cover with plastic wrap; vent.
Microwave on High 5 minutes,
turning dish after 3 minutes. Let
stand, covered, 2 to 3 minutes or
until fish begins to flake when
tested with a fork. Serve with your
favorite accompaniments.

Tuna-Broccoli Casserole

 1 10³/₄-oz. can condensed cream
 of celery soup
¹/₂ cup MIRACLE WHIP Salad
 Dressing
 1 cup (3¹/₂ ozs.) elbow macaroni,
 cooked, drained
 1 cup frozen cut broccoli,
 thawed
 1 6¹/₂-oz. can tuna, drained,
 flaked
¹/₂ cup chopped red or green
 pepper
¹/₄ cup chopped onion
 1 cup shoestring potatoes

Combine soup and salad dressing;
mix well. Add all remaining
ingredients except potatoes; mix
lightly. Spoon into 1-quart
casserole; sprinkle with potatoes.
Bake at 350°, 30 minutes or until
thoroughly heated. Makes 6
servings.

Preparation time: 15 minutes

Baking time: 30 minutes

MICROWAVE: Using 1-quart
microwave-safe casserole, assemble
recipe as directed except for
topping with potatoes; cover.
Microwave on High 6 to 7 minutes
or until thoroughly heated, stirring
after 4 minutes. Stir; sprinkle with
potatoes. Let stand 5 minutes.

Microwave tip: To thaw broccoli,
place frozen broccoli in small
microwave-safe bowl. Cover with
plastic wrap; vent. Microwave on
High 1 to 1¹/₂ minutes or until
thawed.

Cajun Baked Fish

Turkey Tetrazzini

**2/3 cup MIRACLE WHIP Salad
   Dressing**
1/3 cup flour
**1/2 teaspoon celery salt
   Dash of pepper**
2 cups milk
**7 ozs. spaghetti, broken into
   thirds, cooked, drained**
**2 cups chopped cooked turkey
   or chicken**
**3/4 cup (3 ozs.) KRAFT 100%
   Grated Parmesan Cheese**
1 4-oz. can mushrooms, drained
**2 tablespoons chopped pimento
   (optional)**
2 cups fresh bread cubes
**3 tablespoons PARKAY
   Margarine, melted**

Combine salad dressing, flour and
seasonings in medium saucepan.
Gradually add milk. Cook, stirring
constantly, over low heat until
thickened. Add spaghetti, turkey,
1/2 cup cheese, mushrooms and
pimento; mix lightly. Spoon into
2-quart casserole. Toss bread cubes
with margarine and remaining
cheese; top casserole. Bake at 350°,
30 minutes or until lightly
browned. Makes 6 servings.

Preparation time: 30 minutes

Baking time: 30 minutes

Make ahead: Prepare as directed
except for topping with bread cubes
and baking. Cover; chill. When
ready to bake, toss bread cubes
with margarine and remaining
cheese. Top casserole; cover with
foil. Bake at 350°, 25 minutes.
Uncover; continue baking 30
minutes or until lightly browned.

MICROWAVE: Reduce margarine to
2 tablespoons. Microwave
margarine in 2-quart microwave-
safe casserole on High 30 seconds
or until melted. Add bread cubes;
toss. Microwave on High 3 1/2 to 4 1/2
minutes or until crisp, stirring
after 2 minutes. Remove from
casserole; set aside. Combine salad
dressing, flour and seasonings in
same casserole; gradually add
milk. Microwave on High 5 to 6
minutes or until thickened,
stirring after each minute. Stir in
spaghetti, turkey, 1/2 cup cheese,
mushrooms and pimento; mix
lightly. Cover; microwave on High
8 to 10 minutes or until thoroughly
heated, stirring after 5 minutes.
Stir; top with bread cubes. Sprinkle
with remaining cheese. Let stand 5
minutes.

Zesty Reuben
Sandwiches

MIRACLE WHIP Salad Dressing
1 tablespoon chili sauce
1 1/3 cups shredded cabbage
**1 cup (4 ozs.) shredded 100%
   Natural KRAFT Swiss
   Cheese**
**12 rye or pumpernickel bread
   slices**
3/4 lb. corned beef slices

Combine 1/4 cup salad dressing and
chili sauce; mix well. Add cabbage
and cheese; mix lightly. For each
sandwich, cover one bread slice
with cabbage mixture; top with
corned beef and second bread slice.
Spread sandwich with salad
dressing. Grill until lightly
browned on both sides. Makes 6
sandwiches.

Preparation time: 10 minutes

Grilling time: 5 minutes

Hacienda Eggs

6 eggs, beaten
1/2 cup MIRACLE WHIP Salad Dressing
Salsa
2 cups corn chips
1/2 cup chopped green pepper

Combine eggs, salad dressing and 1/4 cup salsa; mix well. Stir in chips and peppers. Pour into greased 9-inch pie plate. Bake at 350°, 20 minutes or until knife inserted in center comes out clean. Serve with sour cream and additional salsa. Top with additional chips, if desired. Makes 6 servings.

Preparation time: 10 minutes

Baking time: 20 minutes

MICROWAVE: Combine ingredients except chips in 1-quart microwave-safe measure or bowl; mix until well blended using wire whisk. Microwave on High 2 minutes, stirring after 1 minute. Stir in chips; pour into greased transparent 9-inch microwave-safe pie plate. Cover with plastic wrap; vent. Microwave on Medium (50%) 9 to 10 minutes or until egg mixture is almost set on bottom. (Lift pie plate to see bottom.) Let stand, covered, 2 minutes. Serve as directed.

Cheesy Corn Frittata

1 1/2 cups cooked rice
1/4 lb. VELVEETA Pasteurized Process Cheese Spread, sliced
3 eggs, beaten
1 8 3/4-oz. can cream style corn
1/2 cup chopped ham
1/3 cup MIRACLE WHIP Salad Dressing
Dash of pepper

Place rice in 10×6-inch baking dish. Top with process cheese spread. Combine remaining ingredients; pour over process cheese spread. Bake at 350°, 30 minutes. Top with additional process cheese spread, sliced, if desired. Let stand 5 minutes before serving. Makes 4 to 6 servings.

Preparation time: 25 minutes

Baking time: 30 minutes plus standing

Make ahead: Prepare recipe as directed except for baking; cover. Refrigerate up to 4 hours. When ready to serve, remove cover. Bake at 350°, 45 minutes. Continue as directed.

MICROWAVE: In 1-quart microwave-safe measure, combine eggs, corn, ham, salad dressing and pepper. Microwave on High 2 minutes, stirring after each minute. Using 10×6-inch microwave-safe dish, assemble recipe as directed. Cover with plastic wrap; vent. Microwave on High 7 to 9 minutes or until almost set, turning dish every 3 minutes. Top with additional process cheese spread, sliced, if desired. Let stand, covered, 5 minutes before serving.

Side Dishes

This chapter has a potpourri of creative cooking ideas, ranging from soups, vegetables and salad dressings to desserts. And a special flair to an otherwise everyday meal with one of these fabulous recipes. Pictured here is Italian Grilled Vegetables; see page 80 for recipe.

Italian Grilled Vegetables

1/2 cup MIRACLE WHIP Salad
  Dressing
1/2 cup KRAFT "Zesty" Italian
  Dressing
2 zucchini, cut in half lengthwise
2 summer squash, cut in half
  lengthwise
2 red, green or yellow peppers,
  cut into quarters

Combine dressings, mixing until well blended. Lightly score cut sides of vegetables; brush one side with salad dressing mixture. Place vegetables, salad dressing side up, on rack of broiler pan. Broil, 4 inches from heat source, 6 minutes. Turn; brush with salad dressing mixture. Continue broiling 6 minutes or until vegetables are tender. Serve with remaining salad dressing mixture. Makes 4 to 6 servings.

Preparation time: 10 minutes

Broiling time: 15 minutes

Variation: Substitute MIRACLE WHIP Light Reduced Calorie Salad Dressing for Regular Salad Dressing.

Easy Carrot Cake

1 two-layer yellow cake mix
1 1/4 cups MIRACLE WHIP Salad
  Dressing
4 eggs
1/4 cup cold water
2 teaspoons ground cinnamon
2 cups finely shredded carrots
1/2 cup chopped walnuts
  Vanilla "Philly" Frosting (recipe
  follows)

In large bowl of electric mixer, combine cake mix, salad dressing, eggs, water and cinnamon, mixing at medium speed until well blended. Stir in carrots and walnuts. Pour into greased 13×9-inch baking pan. Bake 350°, 35 minutes or until wooden pick inserted in center comes out clean. Cool. Frost with Vanilla "Philly" Frosting. Makes 10 to 12 servings.

Preparation time: 25 minutes

Baking time: 35 minutes plus cooling

Vanilla "Philly" Frosting

1 3-oz. pkg. PHILADELPHIA
  BRAND Cream Cheese,
  softened
1 tablespoon milk
1/2 teaspoon vanilla
3 cups sifted powdered sugar

Combine cream cheese, milk and vanilla, mixing until well blended. Gradually add sugar, beating until light and fluffy.

Easy Carrot Cake with Vanilla "Philly" Frosting

Savory Corn Muffins

1 egg, beaten
3/4 cup MIRACLE WHIP Salad Dressing
1 4-oz. can chopped green chilies, drained
1 8¹/₂-oz. pkg. corn muffin mix

Combine egg, salad dressing and chilies, mixing until well blended. Add muffin mix, mixing just until moistened. Spoon into greased medium-size muffin pan, filling each cup 2/3 full. Bake at 400°, 15 minutes. Loosen edge of muffins; remove from pan. Makes 1 dozen.

Preparation time: 10 minutes

Baking time: 15 minutes

Potato Soup with Cheese Crust

4 stalks celery, cut into 2-inch pieces
2 carrots, cut into 2-inch pieces
1 medium potato, peeled, cubed
1 onion, quartered
1 small turnip, peeled, quartered
2¹/₃ cups cold water
1 13³/₄-oz. can chicken broth
1/4 teaspoon black pepper
3/4 cup MIRACLE WHIP Salad Dressing
1/4 teaspoon hot pepper sauce
1 cup (4 ozs.) 100% Natural KRAFT Shredded Sharp Cheddar Cheese
6 slices French or Italian bread, toasted

In food processor work bowl, place celery, carrots, potatoes, onions and turnips; process until vegetables are finely chopped. Spoon vegetable mixture into large saucepan. Add water, broth and pepper. Bring to boil; reduce heat. Simmer 15 minutes, stirring occasionally. Combine 1/4 cup salad dressing and hot pepper sauce. Gradually add salad dressing mixture to hot soup, using wire whisk to blend. Reduce heat to low. Combine remaining salad dressing and 1/2 cup cheese; spread onto toast. Spoon soup into ovenproof bowls; top with toast, cheese side up. Sprinkle with remaining cheese. Broil until golden brown and bubbling hot. Serve immediately. Makes six 1-cup servings.

Preparation time: 30 minutes

Broiling time: 5 minutes

Poppy Seed Dressing

1/2 cup MIRACLE WHIP Salad Dressing
2 tablespoons orange juice
1 tablespoon honey
1 teaspoon grated onion
1 teaspoon poppy seed

Combine ingredients, mixing until well blended. Cover; chill. Makes 3/4 cup.

Preparation time: 5 minutes plus chilling

Variation: Substitute MIRACLE WHIP Light Reduced Calorie Salad Dressing for Regular Salad Dressing.

Blueberry Ice

1 envelope unflavored gelatin
3/4 cup cold water
1/2 cup MIRACLE WHIP Salad
   Dressing
3/4 teaspoon grated lemon peel
3 cups blueberries
3/4 cup sugar

Combine gelatin and water in small saucepan; let stand 1 minute. Stir over low heat until dissolved. Cool. Combine salad dressing and peel; gradually add gelatin, mixing until well blended. Place blueberries in food processor work bowl; process 2 to 3 minutes or until pureed, scraping sides of work bowl as necessary. Add sugar and gelatin mixture; process 2 to 3 minutes or until light and foamy. Pour into 8-inch square baking pan; cover tightly. Freeze until firm. Place in refrigerator 15 minutes before serving. Spoon or scoop into serving dish. Makes 12 servings.

Preparation time: 25 minutes plus freezing

Variations: Omit lemon peel. Substitute 20-oz. pkg. frozen whole strawberries for blueberries.

Substitute MIRACLE WHIP Light Reduced Calorie Salad Dressing for Regular Salad Dressing.

Fruity Ice Cream Dessert

3/4 cup MIRACLE WHIP Salad
   Dressing
1 cup graham cracker crumbs
1 qt. vanilla ice cream, softened
3/4 cup dried mixed fruit
1/4 cup chopped pecans

Combine 1/4 cup salad dressing and crumbs, mixing until well blended. Press onto bottom of 9-inch springform pan. Bake at 350°, 5 minutes. Cool. Combine ice cream, remaining salad dressing, 1/2 cup fruit and pecans; mix well. Spoon over crust. Freeze until firm. Sprinkle with remaining fruit just before serving. Serve in wedges. Makes 10 to 12 servings.

Preparation time: 35 minutes plus freezing

Variation: Substitute 8 or 9-inch square pan for springform pan.

Microwave tip: To soften ice cream, microwave on Medium (50%) 40 seconds, stirring after 20 seconds.

Squash Soup

1 13³/₄-oz. can chicken broth
1 12-oz. pkg. frozen cooked
  winter squash
1 cup carrot slices
¹/₃ cup chopped onion
¹/₄ teaspoon dried basil leaves,
  crushed
³/₄ cup MIRACLE WHIP Salad
  Dressing
1 tablespoon milk

Combine ingredients except salad
dressing and milk in medium
saucepan. Bring to boil. Reduce
heat to medium. Cover; simmer 12
to 15 minutes or until carrots and
onions are tender. Stir in ¹/₂ cup
salad dressing, using wire whisk.
Heat thoroughly, stirring
occasionally. Combine remaining
salad dressing and milk. Spoon
soup into serving bowls; top with
salad dressing mixture. Swirl
gently with spoon. Makes four
1-cup servings.

Preparation time: 30 minutes

MICROWAVE: Substitute one acorn
squash for frozen squash. Pierce
squash several times with a fork.
Microwave whole squash on High 2
minutes. Cut squash in half
lengthwise; remove seeds. Place
squash, cut side up, in shallow
microwave-safe baking dish. Cover
with plastic wrap; vent. Microwave
on High 8 to 10 minutes or until
fork-tender, turning dish every 4
minutes. Let stand 5 minutes.
Scoop out squash; mash. Continue
as directed.

Cajun Potato Topping

¹/₂ cup MIRACLE WHIP Salad
  Dressing
¹/₂ cup sour cream
¹/₄ cup chopped celery
¹/₄ cup chopped onion
¹/₄ cup chopped green pepper
¹/₄ teaspoon garlic powder
¹/₄ teaspoon ground red pepper
¹/₄ teaspoon ground cumin

Combine ingredients; mix well.
Cover; chill. Serve over hot baked
potatoes. Makes 1¹/₂ cups.

Preparation time: 10 minutes plus
chilling

Wild Rice Extravaganza

1 6-oz. pkg. long-grain and wild
  rice
1 4-oz. can mushrooms, drained
¹/₃ cup MIRACLE WHIP Salad
  Dressing

Prepare rice as directed on
package, omitting margarine. Add
mushrooms and salad dressing
during last 5 minutes of cooking.
Let stand 5 minutes before serving.
Makes 6 servings.

Preparation time: 30 minutes plus
standing

Squash Soup

Spinach Bake

2 eggs, beaten
3/4 cup MIRACLE WHIP Salad
   Dressing
2 10-oz. pkgs. frozen chopped
   spinach, thawed, well
   drained
1 14-oz. can artichoke hearts,
   drained, cut into quarters
1/2 cup sour cream
1/4 cup (1 oz.) KRAFT 100%
   Grated Parmesan Cheese
6 crisply cooked bacon slices,
   crumbled

Combine eggs and 1/2 cup salad
dressing, mixing until well
blended. Add spinach and
artichokes; mix lightly. Spoon
mixture into lightly greased
10×6-inch baking dish. Combine
remaining salad dressing, sour
cream and cheese; mix well. Spoon
over spinach mixture. Bake at
350°, 30 minutes or until set.
Sprinkle with bacon. Makes 8
servings.

Preparation time: 10 minutes

Baking time: 30 minutes

MICROWAVE: Substitute 1½-quart
microwave-safe casserole for 10×6-
inch baking dish. Combine eggs
and 1/2 cup salad dressing in
casserole, mixing until well
blended. Add spinach and
artichokes; mix lightly. Microwave
on High 8 to 9 minutes or until
thoroughly heated, stirring every 3
minutes. Combine remaining salad
dressing, sour cream and cheese;
mix well. Spoon over spinach
mixture. Microwave on High 1½ to
2 minutes or until sour cream
mixture is warmed. (Do not over
cook.) Sprinkle with bacon. Let
stand 5 minutes.

Microwave tip: To thaw spinach,
place frozen spinach in 1½-quart
microwave-safe casserole; cover.
Microwave on High 5 minutes.
Break apart with fork; drain well.

Parmesan Potato Crisp

1/2 cup MIRACLE WHIP Salad
   Dressing
5 cups thin unpeeled potato
   slices
3/4 cup (3 ozs.) KRAFT 100%
   Grated Parmesan Cheese
   Pepper (optional)

Generously brush 9-inch pie plate
with salad dressing. Dry potato
slices on paper towel. Arrange one
layer of potatoes, edges slightly
overlapping, on bottom of pie plate.
Brush generously with salad
dressing; sprinkle generously with
cheese. Repeat layers, sprinkling
occasionally with pepper. Bake at
400°, 30 minutes. Cover with foil;
continue baking 30 minutes or
until potatoes are tender.
Immediately invert onto serving
plate. Cut into wedges to serve.
Makes 6 servings.

Preparation time: 10 minutes

Baking time: 1 hour

Variation: Substitute MIRACLE
WHIP Light Reduced Calorie Salad
Dressing for Regular Salad
Dressing.

Cucumber Dressing

1 cup MIRACLE WHIP Salad
  Dressing
1/2 cup shredded cucumber,
  drained, chopped
1/3 cup milk
2 tablespoons chopped parsley
1/4 teaspoon pepper

Combine ingredients; mix well.
Cover; chill. Makes 1½ cups.

Preparation time: 10 minutes plus
chilling

Variation: Substitute MIRACLE
WHIP Light Reduced Calorie Salad
Dressing for Regular Salad
Dressing.

Devilish Good Eggs

6 hard-cooked eggs
1/4 cup MIRACLE WHIP Salad
  Dressing
1 teaspoon KRAFT Pure
  Prepared Mustard
1/8 teaspoon salt

Cut eggs in half. Remove yolks;
mash. Blend in salad dressing,
mustard and salt. Refill whites.
Garnish with parsley and pimento
strips, if desired. Makes 1 dozen.

Preparation time: 25 minutes

Variations: Add one or more of the
following to egg yolk mixture: 1
tablespoon pickle relish, 3 crisply
cooked bacon slices, crumbled, 2
teaspoons chopped chives.

Substitute MIRACLE WHIP Light
Reduced Calorie Salad Dressing for
Regular Salad Dressing.

Garden Vegetables and Rice

3/4 cup cut green beans
3/4 cup thin carrot slices
3 tablespoons green onion slices
1 garlic clove, minced
1 tablespoon oil
1½ cups hot cooked rice
1/3 cup MIRACLE WHIP Salad
  Dressing
2 tablespoons soy sauce
1 tablespoon dry roasted shelled
  sunflower seeds (optional)

Stir-fry beans, carrots, onions and
garlic in oil in large skillet or wok
until crisp-tender. Reduce heat to
medium. Add remaining
ingredients except sunflower seeds;
heat thoroughly, stirring
occasionally. Sprinkle with
sunflower seeds just before serving.
Makes 4 servings.

Preparation time: 25 minutes

Cooking time: 10 minutes

Lemon Cream Dessert

2 cups vanilla wafer crumbs
1 cup MIRACLE WHIP Salad
    Dressing
1 12-oz. container (4½ cups)
    frozen whipped topping,
    thawed
1 6-oz. can frozen lemonade or
    limeade concentrate,
    softened

Combine crumbs and ½ cup salad dressing; mix well. Press mixture onto bottom of 8-inch square baking pan. Bake at 350°, 10 minutes. Cool. Combine remaining ingredients, mixing until well blended. Spoon over crust; cover tightly. Freeze until firm. Place in refrigerator 10 minutes before cutting into squares to serve. Garnish as desired. Makes 9 to 12 servings.

Preparation time: 20 minutes plus freezing

Variation: Substitute strawberry or peach daiquiri frozen concentrate mix for lemonade concentrate.

Black Pepper Dressing

½ cup MIRACLE WHIP Salad
    Dressing
½ cup buttermilk
¾ teaspoon freshly ground black
    pepper

Combine ingredients, mixing until well blended. Cover; chill. Makes 1 cup.

Preparation time: 5 minutes plus chilling

Golden Twice-Baked Potatoes

4 large baking potatoes, baked
1½ cups (6 ozs.) 100% Natural
    KRAFT Shredded Sharp
    Cheddar Cheese
⅓ cup MIRACLE WHIP Salad
    Dressing
¼ cup milk
2 tablespoons green onion slices
4 crisply cooked bacon slices,
    crumbled

Slice tops from potatoes; scoop out center, leaving ⅛-inch shell. Mash potatoes. Add 1 cup cheese, salad dressing and milk; beat until fluffy. Spoon into shells. Place on ungreased cookie sheet. Top with remaining cheese, onions and bacon. Bake at 350°, 15 minutes. Makes 4 servings.

Preparation time: 1 hour 20 minutes

Baking time: 15 minutes

MICROWAVE: Prepare filling and spoon into potatoes as directed. Place in 12×8-inch microwave-safe baking dish. Microwave on High 7 to 8 minutes or until thoroughly heated, turning dish after 4 minutes. Top with remaining cheese, onions and bacon. Microwave on High 1½ to 2 minutes or until cheese is melted.

Microwave tip: To cook potatoes, pierce and place on paper towel. Microwave on High 15 to 18 minutes or until tender, turning and rearranging potatoes after 8 minutes. Let stand 5 minutes.

Lemon Cream Dessert

Traditional Sage Stuffing

1 cup MIRACLE WHIP Salad Dressing
¾ cup cold water
2 teaspoons poultry seasoning
2 teaspoons ground sage
½ teaspoon ground marjoram
¼ cup PARKAY Margarine
1 cup chopped celery
1 cup chopped onion
½ cup chopped mushrooms
1 12-oz. bag unseasoned stuffing mix
6 crisply cooked bacon slices, crumbled

Combine salad dressing, water and seasonings; mix well. Set aside. Melt margarine. Add celery, onions and mushrooms; cook until tender. Combine vegetable mixture, stuffing mix and bacon; mix lightly. Stir in salad dressing mixture. Spoon into 3-quart casserole or 13×9-inch baking dish; cover. Bake at 350°, 30 minutes. Makes 6 cups.

Preparation time: 25 minutes

Baking time: 30 minutes

Variations: Substitute ⅔ cup apple juice for water.

Substitute 1½ teaspoons dried thyme leaves, crushed, for poultry seasoning.

Omit onions. Add ½ cup chopped apple and ⅓ cup chopped nuts to stuffing mixture just before baking.

MICROWAVE: Prepare salad dressing mixture as directed. Microwave margarine in 3-quart microwave-safe casserole on High 1 minute or until melted. Add vegetables; microwave on High 5 to 6 minutes or until tender, stirring after 3 minutes. Add salad dressing mixture, stuffing and bacon; mix lightly. Microwave on High 10 minutes or until thoroughly heated, stirring every 5 minutes.

Zesty Thousand Island Dressing

1 cup MIRACLE WHIP Salad Dressing
½ cup chopped celery
¼ cup chopped green pepper
¼ cup finely chopped onion
¼ cup chili sauce
1 hard-cooked egg, chopped
1 teaspoon Worcestershire sauce

Combine ingredients; mix well. Cover; chill. Makes 2 cups.

Preparation time: 25 minutes plus chilling

Variation: Substitute MIRACLE WHIP Light Reduced Calorie Salad Dressing for Regular Salad Dressing.

Tasty Vegetable Medley

1 10³/₄-oz. can condensed cream
  of mushroom soup
¹/₃ cup MIRACLE WHIP Salad
  Dressing
1 16-oz. bag frozen mixed
  vegetables, thawed, drained
1 2.8-oz. can French fried onions

Combine soup and salad dressing;
mix well. Stir in vegetables and
half of onions. Spoon into 1-quart
casserole. Bake at 350°, 30
minutes or until thoroughly
heated. Sprinkle with remaining
onions; continue baking 5 minutes.
Makes 5 servings.

Preparation time: 5 minutes

Baking time: 35 minutes

MICROWAVE: Substitute 1¹/₂-quart
microwave-safe casserole for
1-quart casserole. Combine soup
and salad dressing in 1¹/₂-quart
microwave-safe casserole. Stir in
vegetables and half of onions;
cover. Microwave on High 7 to 8
minutes or until thoroughly
heated, stirring after 4 minutes.
Stir; sprinkle with remaining
onions. Microwave, uncovered, on
High 1 minute.

Make ahead: Prepare recipe as
directed except for baking. Cover;
chill. When ready to serve, remove
cover. Bake at 350°, 30 minutes or
until thoroughly heated. Continue
as directed.

Microwave tip: To thaw vegetables,
place in 1¹/₂-quart microwave-safe
casserole; cover. Microwave on
Medium (50%) 10 to 12 minutes or
until thawed, stirring after 5
minutes.

Cucumber-Dill Potato Topping

¹/₂ cup MIRACLE WHIP Salad
  Dressing
¹/₂ cup plain yogurt
¹/₂ cup chopped cucumber
¹/₂ teaspoon dill weed

Combine ingredients; mix well.
Cover; chill. Serve over hot baked
potatoes. Makes 1¹/₃ cups.

Preparation time: 5 minutes plus
chilling

Variation: Substitute MIRACLE
WHIP Light Reduced Calorie Salad
Dressing for Regular Salad
Dressing

Parmesan-Chive Potato Topping

¹/₂ cup MIRACLE WHIP Salad
  Dressing
¹/₂ cup sour cream
¹/₄ cup (1 oz.) KRAFT 100%
  Grated Parmesan Cheese
1 teaspoon chopped chives

Combine ingredients; mix well.
Cover; chill. Serve over hot baked
potatoes. Makes 1 cup.

Preparation time: 5 minutes plus
chilling

Variation: Substitute MIRACLE
WHIP Light Reduced Calorie Salad
Dressing for Regular Salad
Dressing and plain yogurt for sour
cream.

Chewy Double Chocolate Brownies

2 eggs, beaten
½ cup MIRACLE WHIP Salad Dressing
¼ cup cold water
1 21.5-oz. pkg. fudge brownie mix
1 6-oz. pkg. semi-sweet chocolate pieces

Combine eggs, salad dressing and water; mix well. Stir in brownie mix, mixing just until moistened. Add chocolate pieces; mix lightly. Pour into greased 13×9-inch baking pan. Bake at 350°, 30 minutes or until edges begin to pull away from sides of pan. Cool; sprinkle with sifted powdered sugar, if desired. Cut into squares. Makes approximately 2 dozen.

Preparation time: 5 minutes

Baking time: 30 minutes plus cooling

Lemony Fruit Topping

½ cup MIRACLE WHIP Light Reduced Calorie Salad Dressing
½ cup lemon flavored yogurt

Combine ingredients; mix well. Cover; chill. Serve over fresh fruit. Makes 1 cup.

Preparation time: 5 minutes plus chilling.

Variation: Substitute MIRACLE WHIP Salad Dressing for Reduced Calorie Salad Dressing.

Coleslaw Dressing

¼ cup milk
½ cup MIRACLE WHIP Salad Dressing
1 tablespoon vinegar
½ teaspoon KRAFT Pure Prepared Mustard

Gradually add milk to salad dressing, mixing until blended. Stir in remaining ingredients. Makes ¾ cup.

Preparation time: 5 minutes

Variation: Substitute MIRACLE WHIP Light Reduced Calorie Salad Dressing for Regular Salad Dressing.

Fruit Dip

½ cup MIRACLE WHIP Salad Dressing
2 tablespoons KRAFT Apricot, Peach, Pineapple or Red Raspberry Preserves
1 cup thawed frozen whipped topping

Combine salad dressing and preserves; mix well. Fold in whipped topping. Serve with assorted fruit dippers. Makes 1⅓ cups.

Preparation time: 5 minutes

Chewy Double Chocolate Brownies

Index